Government in Arkansas

Eighth Edition

Douglas L. Reed
Margaret M. Reed
Editors

League of Women Voters of Arkansas

Copyright© 1976, 1979, 1983, 1989, 1993, 2004, 2009
League of Women Voters Arkansas
All rights reserved

No part of this work may be reproduced or transmitted in any form or by any means - electronic or mechanical - including photocopying and recording or by any information storage or retrieval system without the written permission of The League of Women Voters Arkansas unless such copying is expressly permitted by federal copyright law. Address inquiries regarding permissions to reproduce or transmit to the League of Women Voters Arkansas, 2020 West 3rd Street, Suite 315-C, Little Rock, AR 72205.

First printing..	November 1976
Second printing, with revisions..	June 1979
Third printing...	July 1979
Fourth printing, with revisions...	January 1983
Fifth printing, with revisions..	August 1989
Sixth printing, with revisions...	September 1993
Seventh printing, with revisions...	August 2004
Eighth printing, with revisions...	August 2009

To Place an Order

Educators Book Depository of Arkansas, Inc.
6700 Sloane Drive
Little Rock, AR 72206

Order by Phone
(501) 490-0007

Order Online
http://www.educatorsbook.com

Order by Fax
(501) 490-0006

Order by E-Mail
books@educatorsbook.com

Printed by Lightning Source, Inc., 1246 Heil Quaker Blvd., La Vergne, TN 37086

Contents

Tables, Maps, and Figures... iv

Introduction.. v

Foreword... vii

Abbreviations and Definitions... viii

Historical Background.. ix

Chapter 1 – The Arkansas Constitution... 1

Chapter 2 – The Legislative Branch... 7

Chapter 3 – The Governor and Other Constitutional Officers............. 29

Chapter 4 – The State Bureaucracy... 39

Chapter 5 – The Judicial Branch... 51

Chapter 6 – Local Government... 67

Chapter 7 – Political Parties and Interest Groups............................. 85

Chapter 8 – Elections.. 95

Chapter 9 – Education.. 111

Chapter 10 – Finance... 129

Appendix A – Amendments to the Arkansas Constitution of 1874........ 147

Appendix B – Arkansas Governors.. 151

Appendix C – Important Dates in Arkansas' Political History............. 153

Appendix D – Arkansas Congressional Districts................................ 155

Bibliographic References.. 157

Index.. 159

Tables, Maps, and Figures

TABLES
Arkansas Constitution of 1874... 3
Comparison of Arkansas Constitution to U.S. Constitution.....................4
Bills Filed and Laws Enacted in Regular Sessions since 1961.................12
General Assembly Committees...19
Arkansas Circuit Courts..61
U.S. Constitutional Amendments Regarding the Right to Vote.............. 95
Arkansas Elections..104
Four-Year Public Universities in Arkansas... 125
Two-Year Public Colleges in Arkansas..126
Independent Colleges and Universities in Arkansas.............................127
Total State Revenues 131
Total State Expenditures 135
County Ad Valorem Millage Allowable under Arkansas Constitution.......... 138
Municipal Ad Valorem Millage Allowable under Arkansas Constitution... 140

MAPS
State Representative Districts... 10
State Senate Districts.. 11
Circuit Court Districts.. 60
Arkansas Congressional Districts..155

FIGURES
How a Bill Becomes a Law... 15
Initiative, Referendum, Referral, and Recall in Arkansas...................... 26
Arkansas Court Structure... 59

APPENDIX
A. Amendments to the Constitution of 1874...................................... 147
B. Governors of Arkansas..151
C. Important Dates in Arkansas Political History.............................. 153
D. Arkansas Congressional Districts... 155

Introduction

The League of Women Voters of Arkansas (LWVAR) was established in September, 1955, through the grassroots efforts of county and city Leagues of Women Voters throughout Arkansas. The League of Women Voters of the United States (LWVUS), which was born of the Women's Suffrage movement in 1920, is the national umbrella organization which establishes the framework, policies and procedures for state and local Leagues. All 50 states have incorporated state chapters along with the District of Columbia and the Virgin Islands. In addition, each state has several county/parish and city chapters under its leadership.

The League of Women Voters Arkansas is a non-governmental organization (NGO) receiving no local, state, or federal funding. It relies solely on the generosity of its membership and friends to support its operations and activities. The League is a non-partisan, political organization that encourages the informed and active participation of citizens in all levels of government. Our vision is to make democracy work through citizen engagement, advocacy and voter education.

Government in Arkansas is a valuable resource for the citizens of our state. It was first written by Peg Anderson of Fayetteville, Arkansas. Having served as the editor of four subsequent printings, Ms. Anderson provided an excellent road map for the current and future updates. Dr. Douglas Reed and Margaret Reed have updated and enhanced the eighth edition of *Government in Arkansas*, tailoring it to use in the classroom for history, social studies and civics. The League of Women Voters finds that elected officials, candidates seeking election, librarians as well as a multitude of citizens who are interested in understanding the structure and functions of government in Arkansas use this resource to carry out their interests in a participatory and democratic government. The League of Women Voters of Arkansas as well as local and county Leagues also publish the *Guide to Elected Officials* and the *Arkansas Citizens' Information Guide*.

It is an honor to publish the eighth edition of *Government in Arkansas* through the diligence and expertise of Douglas and Margaret Reed as well as the determination of the Board of Directors of the League of Women Voters of Arkansas. We all share in the excitement of the publication of this up-to-date and well-researched edition of *Government in Arkansas*.

Sincerely,
Mary Alice Serafini, President
League of Women Voters Arkansas

Foreword

Throughout its existence, *Government in Arkansas* has sought to enhance citizens' understanding of state and local government. Our goal in editing this new edition has been to continue the efforts of Peg Anderson, the original author and a founding leader of the League of Women Voters of Arkansas.

This edition includes updated information since 2004 along with an instructional resources CD for teachers.

We sincerely appreciate various university colleagues for serving as reviewers: Hal Bass, Ouachita Baptist University; Teddy Davis, Arkansas State University at Beebe; Arthur English, University of Arkansas at Little Rock; and Judy Tobler, Northwest Arkansas Community College.

Several board members from the League of Women Voters of Arkansas also played an important role, particularly in the areas of proofreading and handling administrative aspects of the publication: Stephanie Johnson, Linda Okiror, Marion Orton, and Libby Wheeler.

Ultimately, we could not have completed this edition without the contributions of these persons. We hope *Government in Arkansas* will be a useful reference tool for those who seek to learn more about Arkansas governmental structure and functions.

Douglas L. Reed and Margaret M. Reed
Co-Editors

Abbreviations and Definitions

Amend.	Amendment to the Arkansas or U.S. Constitutions
A.C.A.	Arkansas Code Annotated
etc.	(et cetera) and so forth
ff.	and following
FY	Fiscal Year (July 1 – June 30)
p.	page
pp.	pages
Sec.	Section of Arkansas or U.S. Constitutions
V, 3	Article V, Section 3 of the Arkansas Constitution
ad valorem	according to value
certiorari	a writ issued from a superior court calling up the record of a proceeding in an inferior court for review
de novo	from the beginning
en banc	as a full court; with all judges present
ex officio	by virtue of an office held
habeas corpus	a writ requiring a person to be brought before a judge
mandamus	a writ from a superior court to an inferior court commanding that a specified thing be done
per capita	for each person
per diem	for each day
pro tempore	(a legal proceeding to determine) by what authority (one has an office or a liberty)
sine die	without a fixing a day (for future action)

Historical Background

Arkansas has an interesting political history, filled with colorful individuals and influenced by important social and historical events. From the politics of Native American migrants seeking land for settlement to the civil rights movement, Arkansas has been affected by geographic, socio-economic, and international concerns.

The earliest political activities involved several Native America tribes attempting to maintain or expand their tribal holdings. The major tribes were the Caddo, Osage, and Quapaw. According to analysts, only the Caddo tribe did not migrate into the land that was to become Arkansas. (Greer and Cole, 1991: 61)

The next major political influence was the politics of empire. Initially, Spanish and French explorers claimed the area of present-day Arkansas for their nations. Although scholars debate his exact route, Spanish conquistador Hernando de Soto explored portions of Arkansas in 1541-1543. In addition, Frenchman Henri de Tonti, a lieutenant of Robert de La Salle, founded a settlement in 1686. (Arnold, 1991: 5)

The turn of the 19th Century marked a significant change in Arkansas history. Control and governance of the land area now known as Arkansas shifted from the Europeans to the United States. The Louisiana Purchase of 1803 gave the U.S. legal claim to this land area and encouraged the country's westward expansion. President Thomas Jefferson sent Meriwether Lewis and James Clark to determine the northern boundary of the Purchase. Jefferson commissioned William Dunbar and George Hunter to explore the southern portion of the Purchase, which included the Arkansas Territory. (Whayne, et. al., 2002: 79-87)

After being part of the Indiana, Louisiana, and Missouri Territories, the Arkansas Territory was formally established when President James Monroe signed an act of Congress on March 1, 1819. The first territorial capital was at Arkansas Post, located at the eastern edge of the Arkansas Territory near present-day Gould. At their first meeting, members of the Arkansas Territory Legislature lobbied to change the capital's location, in part because the area around Arkansas Post was swampland full of mosquitoes and prone to flooding. In addition, members felt the capital should be in the center of the territory, making it more accessible to settlers. After a series of turnovers among the political leadership, the territorial government stabilized and finally moved the capital to Little Rock in June, 1821, which had been discovered by explorer Bernard de la Harpe nearly 100 years earlier. (Bolton, 1998: 24-28; Dougan, 1994: 67)

Arkansas statehood relied more upon external than internal political factors. National political efforts to balance the number of slave and non-slave states was the prime element in Arkansas' admission as the 25th state. In 1836, Arkansas was admitted as a slave state and Michigan entered the Union as a free state.

The Civil War of the mid-1800s prompted Arkansas to make a pivotal decision that would leave an indelible mark on its political history – whether to stay in the

Union. Several political factions waged a serious struggle over the secession question. Some actors wanted Arkansas to follow the path of the border states, such as Missouri and Maryland, and delay the secession decision. Others encouraged immediate action by the state to join the Confederacy. The initial efforts for secession failed, but ultimately Arkansas joined with the Deep South and voted for secession in 1861.

The Reconstruction period (1865-1874) was marred by corruption and a failure to dramatically improve the welfare of the newly freed slaves. This era, however, did produce some long-standing political characteristics, including the electoral dominance of the Democratic Party.

Another vestige of Reconstruction is the state's Constitution of 1874. This document remains the core governing authority for the state and is characterized by efforts to limit governmental actions. In fact, many of its provisions focus on reducing the actions available to political decision-makers.

The Great Depression of the 1930s created a new dynamic in Arkansas politics. Much like the rest of the country, average citizens began to accept an increasing role of the central government. For the first time many Arkansans were affected directly by federal programs. Also, President Franklin D. Roosevelt's New Deal efforts helped the Democratic Party maintain its dominance of Arkansas political life.

A primary political issue in the post-World War II era was civil rights. Arkansas' record on civil rights is similar to most southern states. The state consistently failed to uphold policies and take actions that would result in equality for its African-American citizens. The Little Rock Central High School crisis illustrates vividly the political struggle over desegregation efforts. In 1957, President Dwight D. Eisenhower ordered National Guard Troops and the 101st Airborne Division to provide safe passage and entry of nine African-American students into Central High. This action overrode efforts by Arkansas Governor Orval Faubus to maintain segregation. (Johnson, 2000: 139-40)

Another characteristic of Arkansas politics in the post-WWII time period has been the selection of progressive political office-holders, such as Senator J. William Fulbright, former Governor and U.S. Senator Dale Bumpers, former Governor and U.S. Senator David Pryor, and former Governor and President Bill Clinton. Although change has been slow, revisions in education policy, economic development strategies, and government structure have occurred. Another feature altering the political landscape is the economic growth and population expansion in Northwest Arkansas. This seems to be a major influence on the political and economic power bases within the state.

At the beginning of the 21st century, Arkansas faced many of the same issues that have influenced its past. These concerns included: provision for an adequate public education; expansion of employment opportunities; and creation of an efficient government structure. Efforts to address these and other policy questions continue to make the Arkansas political scene a fascinating and worthwhile area of study.

The Arkansas Constitution

Constitutional History

Arkansas' constitutional history consists of five different constitutions. Their adoption dates were 1836, 1861, 1864, 1868, and 1874.

To qualify for statehood, Arkansas wrote its first constitution in 1836. Some controversy surrounded this constitution because territorial representatives drafted it before statehood was actually granted. When Arkansas seceded and joined the Confederacy, the state approved a new constitution in 1861. Known as the "Confederate Constitution," it retained much of the 1836 provisions. The primary difference was that references to the "United States of America" were changed to the "Confederate States of America."

As the Civil War progressed, Union forces occupied more territory in the state. This change in political fortune meant that many individuals who opposed secession were now in positions of influence. Ultimately, these events lead to the call for a new constitution. Twenty-four counties sent delegates to a constitutional convention held in Little Rock in January 1864. The convention adopted a new constitution for the state. For a time, the state had two governments in operation: the Union government in Little Rock based on the newly adopted constitution and a Confederate government in Washington, Arkansas, utilizing the 1861 Constitution.

After the Civil War, the U.S. Congress declared the existing Southern governments illegal. The 1868 or "Radical Reconstruction Constitution" was created in response to this congressional edict. Moreover, many of the delegates to this convention were not native Arkansans. The 1868 Constitution was characterized by a dramatic centralization of power, particularly in the executive branch. Some analysts contend this was essential, because the war's devastation meant many local governments lacked the ability to implement necessary functions. Another criticism was the issue of taxes. Arkansans at the time considered the tax burden excessive and felt the system worked

Chapter 1

In This Chapter

Constitutional History

Constitution of 1874

Constitutional Amendment Process

Comparison to Other States

Terms to Know

amendment

Confederacy

constitution

initiative process

ratification

Reconstruction

secede

statute

to their disadvantage. Assessors appointed by the governor received a percentage of levied taxes, thus the tax collectors had an incentive to maintain high assessment levels. Another problem with the Reconstruction Constitution was political corruption. Many citizens voiced concern about the government wasting public funds.

Over time, more Arkansans began to take the oath of allegiance required under Reconstruction provisions. This enabled them to regain their right to register and vote. As their numbers increased, they began to demand a new constitution that would address governmental power and taxation issues. By 1874, the state legislature responded to citizen concerns and submitted an act calling for a new constitutional convention. The voters overwhelmingly approved this act, leading to Arkansas' fifth and current constitution. (Barnhart, 1973: 2-5 in Nunn ed.)

Constitution of 1874

The original Arkansas Constitution of 1874 contained 19 articles. The chairman of the constitutional convention appointed nineteen standing committees and much of the committees' efforts correspond to the constitutional articles. Today's amended version has 20 articles. The Constitution was designed to address the immediate concerns of Arkansans. These problems included centralization of power, political corruption, taxation, and other issues associated with Reconstruction. The document reflected the citizenry's high level of distrust for government. Because of this approach, historian Walter Nunn has argued the general tone of the Arkansas Constitution is "negativism." (Nunn, 1973: 21-25) That is, the authors attempted to limit and control governmental power to prevent the excesses they had witnessed under the 1868 Constitution.

The 1874 Constitution dramatically increases the number of elective offices to address the issues of centralization of power and representation. In addition, the elective office terms were shortened from four to two years. This gave voters an estimated 44 opportunities to vote on officeholders every four years, compared to the 14 times available in the 1868 Constitution. Also, this change removed a great deal of executive appointive power. (Blair, 1997: 122)

The 1874 Constitution also takes steps to control political corruption. The primary tool in this effort is detailed statutes that guide government behavior. For example, constitutional provisions provide specific directives on conducting elections; building or repairing public buildings; purchasing stationery; and furnishing the hall and rooms for the General Assembly (Art. XIX).

Taxation and spending are other issues the 1874 Constitution addresses. In fact, about one-fourth of the document focuses on financial issues. Arkansas political analyst Peg Anderson, founding member of the League of Women Voters of

Arkansas, argues this reflected the convention delegates' desire to correct the conditions that had lead to bribery, high taxes, embezzlement, and a large state debt. At the state level, tax and appropriation laws require extraordinary majority votes in the legislature. Also, local government taxing power is strictly limited. Here again, the delegates were responding to the political shortcomings they had experienced under the previous constitution.

In addition to this libertarianism, the Constitution of 1874 does have several positive features. The writers were careful to include democratic principles of government. Moreover, the dramatic increase in elective positions and frequency of elections gave average citizens greater potential influence over political officeholders. In addition, the document enumerates the basic rights of individuals in the Declaration of Rights (Art. II). The Declaration of Rights combines the basic philosophy of the Declaration of Independence with the U.S. Constitution's Bill of Rights. The rights expressed in the state's constitution provide a greater elaboration of a citizen's civil protections. This was especially important before the U.S. Supreme Court's actions that incorporated much of the national Bill of Rights protections to the states.

Arkansas Constitution of 1874	
Articles	
---	Preamble
I	Boundaries
II	Declaration of Rights (29 sections)
III	Franchise and Elections (12 sections)
IV	Departments (2 sections)
V	Legislative Department (41 sections)
VI	Executive Department (23 sections)
VII	Judiciary (52 sections)
VIII	Apportionment (6 sections)
IX	Exemptions (10 sections)
X	Agriculture, Mining, and Manufacturing (3 sections)
XI	Militia (4 sections)
XII	Municipal and Private Corporations (12 sections)
XIII	Counties (5 sections)
XIV	Education (4 sections)
XV	Impeachment and Address (3 sections)
XVI	Finance and Taxation (16 sections)
XVII	Railroads, Canals, and Turnpikes (13 sections)
XVIII	Judicial Circuits
XIX	Miscellaneous Provisions (27 sections)
XX	Holford Bonds Not To Be Paid
---	Schedule
Source: Arkansas Secretary of State	

Constitutional Amendment Process

Arkansas' constitutional amendment process is similar to those of the U.S. Constitution and most other states. The Arkansas Constitution may be amended either by the legislature or a citizen initiative.

Under Section 22 of Article 19, the General Assembly may propose up to three amendments per ballot, each listed separately. The amendment requires majority approval of both houses in a recorded vote, publication in at least one newspaper in each county for six months prior to the next election of the Assembly, and majority approval of the voters.

Under Section 1 of Article 5 (as amended by Amendment 7), 10% of legal voters may propose an amendment by initiative, requiring majority approval of the voters. The proposed amendment must be filed with the Arkansas Secretary of State not less than four months before the election. Thirty days prior to the election, the petitioners (at their own expense) must publish the amendment "in some paper of general circulation." Unlike legislative amendments, there are no limits on the number of amendments by initiative that may be proposed on any one ballot.

Comparison to Other States

Most state constitutions are criticized for being too long and too specific, requiring frequent amendment, and lacking political effectiveness. The Arkansas constitution is subject to all of these criticisms. The state's constitution has nearly 60,000 words compared to the U.S. Constitution's 8,700 words. Only four states have constitutions longer than Arkansas.

Comparison of Arkansas Constitution to U.S. Constitution			
Characteristics	Arkansas Constitution	United States Constitution	50-State Average
Length (words)	59,500	8,700	37,436
Amendments	83	27	143
Source: *The Book of the States*, 2008, p. 10			

As noted earlier, the Arkansas Constitution includes explicit details concerning elections, contracts for public works, taxing, and spending. A lengthy, specific document tends to be plagued by contradictions, and this leads to the need for frequent amendment.

All state constitutions include provisions that allow them to be amended or replaced with a new document. Arkansas law allows both of these constitutional reform methods. Arkansans have attempted to completely replace the Constitution of 1874 on several occasions. Constitutional conventions formally proposed new constitutions in 1918, 1970, and 1980, but the citizens rejected these efforts. Therefore, the only constitutional changes since 1874 have been the result of the formal amending process.

Regarding amendments put forth by the legislature, Arkansas is among 17 states that require a simple majority vote in both chambers to propose amendments. All other states require an extraordinary majority vote in both houses of three-fifths, two-thirds, or three-fourths. Amending by citizen initiative petition is the less common procedure; Arkansas is one of only 18 states that allow this method of constitutional amendment.

One concern associated with state constitutions is political effectiveness. Another concern is limiting the power of the state in order to protect people's rights. Efficient government and protecting individual rights are, in many cases, conflicting goals. The Arkansas Constitution limits the governor by having many executive officials elected rather than appointed by the chief executive. Moreover, local governments were very limited in their independent financial activities. These and other restrictions are common among the states. Arkansas, like other states, will continue to work on the balance between giving decision-makers enough power to effectively do their jobs, while providing safeguards to ensure leaders do not abuse their power.

Overall, one should not be too critical of those who wrote the 1874 Constitution. This document was in direct response to the political events of the time. The citizenry experienced abuse of political power due to centralization of authority. Also, Arkansans believed the state's taxation system worked to their disadvantage. The constitution was responsive to these and other concerns. Noted Arkansas political scientist Diane Blair observed, "… the 1874 constitution does seem to have genuinely reflected the will of the people." She goes on to argue that unlike the previous state constitutions, the 1874 constitution was authorized and ratified by a representative segment of the Arkansas population. (Blair, 1997: 123) Therefore, the state's constitution can best be understood in its historical context.

Additional Resources

Arkansas Constitution of 1874 (interactive web site)
http://www.sos.arkansas.gov/ar-constitution/arconst/arconst.htm

Arkansas Constitution of 1874 (PDF document)
http://www.arkleg.state.ar.us/assembly/Summary/ArkansasConstitution1874.pdf

The Legislative Branch

Chapter 2

Following the national legislative model, Arkansas' legislative branch consists of a Senate and House of Representatives, collectively known as the Arkansas General Assembly.

Senate

The Senate is comprised of 35 members, each elected from a single-member district. Senators serve staggered four-year terms with one-half of the senators elected every two years. Since the Board of Apportionment redraws the senate district lines following each decennial census, senators draw lots to determine which senators will get four-year terms and which will get two-year terms. This is done at the beginning of the regular General Assembly session following their election. The lieutenant governor serves *ex officio* as president of the Senate and is its presiding officer. The lieutenant governor does not participate in debate and votes only to break a tie. At each regular session of the General Assembly, the Senate elects a president *pro tempore* from its own membership who is second in line of succession to the office of the governor in the event of death, resignation, or absence from the state of the governor and lieutenant governor. Senate members also elect a secretary of the Senate, who is not a member of the Senate, but who is responsible for administrative and clerical duties of this body.

House of Representatives

The House of Representatives consists of 100 members elected from 100 House districts. Beginning in 2000, all House members are elected from single-member districts. This is a change from previous legislatures where some representatives were chosen from multi-member districts. Representatives serve two-year terms.

Presiding over the House is the speaker, who is elected by House members. At every regular session, a caucus of the entire membership is called for the purpose of selecting by secret ballot

In This Chapter
Senate
House of Representatives
Qualifications
Apportionment
Sessions
Composition of the General Assembly
Term Limits
Vacancies
Legislative Procedures and Rules
Committee Organization
Interim Organization of the General Assembly
Bureau of Legislative Research
Initiative and Referendum
Comparison to Other States

Terms to Know
appropriation
bill
clincher motion
initiative
referendum
resolution
term limits

a member of the House to be speaker-designate. A majority vote is required for election. In case no member receives a majority vote, a run-off is held between the two top candidates. The speaker-designate serves as the speaker at the following regular session unless unable to do so because of resignation, death, or failure to be reelected. In such case, a speaker is chosen by the membership upon the convening of that session. The speaker serves until January 1 of the calendar year that a new General Assembly meets at which time the speaker vacates his office to allow the speaker-designate the privilege of the use of the office.

At the beginning of each session, the speaker appoints a member of the House to serve as speaker *pro tempore* to preside in the absence of the speaker. The speaker may also appoint assistant speaker *pro tempores* - one from each of the existing congressional districts. Other officers of the House are the chief clerk, who is appointed by the speaker-designate and is custodian of all bills, papers, and records of the House; the parliamentarian; and the chaplain.

Qualifications

Senators are required to be at least 25 years of age. Representatives must be at least 21. Both senators and representatives must be United States citizens, residents of Arkansas for not less than two years and residents of their districts for not less than one year. The Arkansas Constitution places further restrictions on those who desire to be candidates for the House or Senate, including:

- "No judge of the supreme, circuit, or inferior courts of law or equity, Secretary of State, Attorney-General for the State, Auditor or Treasurer, recorder, or clerk of any court of record, sheriff, coroner, member of Congress, nor any other person holding any lucrative office under the United States or this State (militia officers, justices of the peace, postmasters, officers of public schools and notaries excepted), shall be eligible to a seat in either house of the General Assembly."
  (V, 7)
- "No person hereafter convicted of embezzlement of public money, bribery, forgery or other infamous crime shall be eligible to [serve in] the General Assembly...." (V, 9)
- "A member expelled for corruption shall not thereafter be eligible to [serve in] either house..."(V, 12)
- "No senator or representative may, during his or her term of office, be appointed or elected to any civil office under the state." (V, 10)

Apportionment

The Arkansas Constitution requires that the membership of the House and the Senate be reapportioned every ten years following the taking of the federal census. Apportioning (analyzing population changes) and redistricting (re-drawing legislative district boundaries based on population changes) are done in Arkansas by the State Board of Apportionment, which consists of the governor (chairman), attorney general, and secretary of state. The United States Supreme Court has ruled that all districts must conform to the principle of "one person-one vote," and that all districts be of substantially equal population size. The board also gives consideration to factors such as geography and county and city lines. Racial factors are also considered since U.S. congressional legislation and legal challenges have resulted in the courts requiring creation of districts with African American voting-age majorities.

Sessions

In the general election of 2008, Arkansans voted in favor of a constitutional amendment that changed state legislative sessions from a biennial basis (meets every other year) to an annual basis (meets every year). The amendment also gives legislators the authority to decide the purpose and the length of annual sessions. Regular sessions begin in January and end in April.

In recent years during regular sessions, the General Assembly has tended to introduce and pass large numbers of bills. One reason is a constitutional provision that requires that "all other appropriations shall be made by separate bills, each embracing but one subject." (V, 30) Therefore, except for the general appropriation bill (covers the operation of executive, legislative, and judicial branches), appropriations for all boards, commissions, departments, and agencies are treated separately. Another reason may be that legislators are responsive to the requests of their constituents on matters large and small.

The governor may call special sessions by proclamation. Items specified by the governor must be considered first, but following completion of the business in the governor's call, the General Assembly may, by a two-thirds vote of both houses, consider other matters.

State Representative Districts

Source: Arkansas House of Representatives

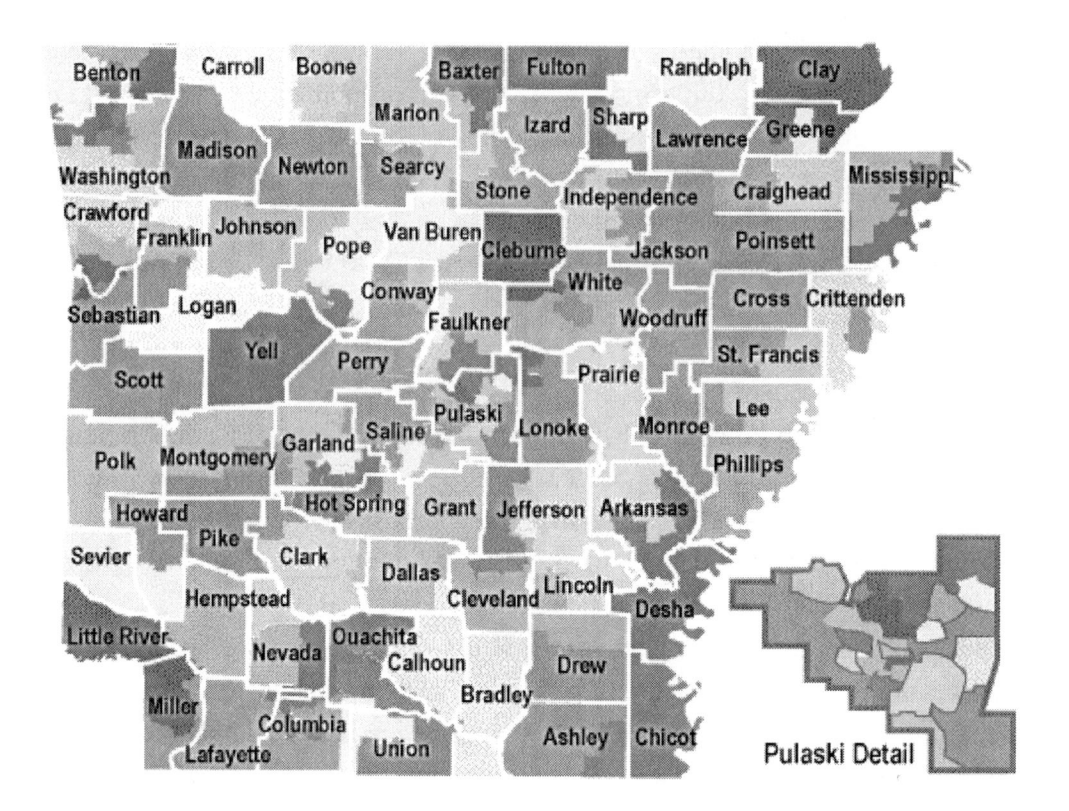

State Senate Districts

Source: Arkansas Senate

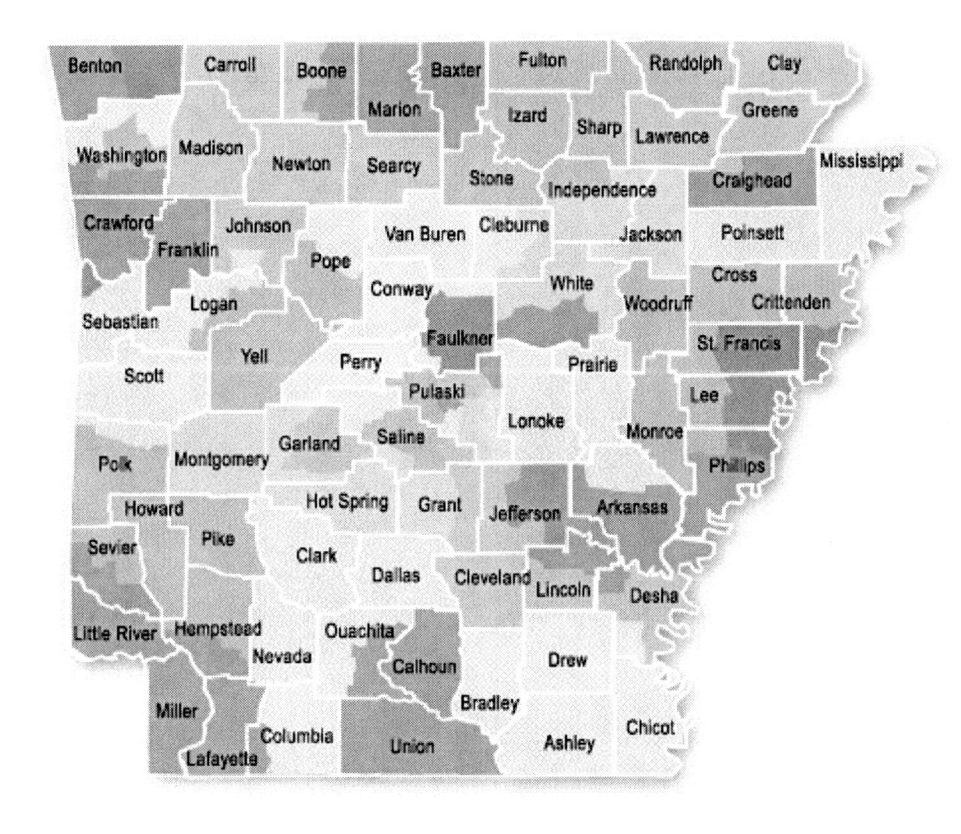

Bills Filed and Laws Enacted in Regular Sessions Since 1961				
Session Year	House Bills	Senate Bills	Total Bills Introduced	Laws Enacted	Percent Enacted
1961	579	402	981	505	51%
1963	615	366	981	559	57%
1965	677	386	1,063	577	54%
1967	739	491	1,230	658	53%
1969	804	532	1,336	699	52%
1971	840	579	1,417	829	59%
1973	976	661	1,637	894	55%
1975	1,248	852	2,100	1,239	59%
1977	961	633	1,594	958	60%
1979	1,202	765	1,967	1,118	57%
1981	1,018	629	1,647	1,120	68%
1983	1,011	572	1,583	937	59%
1985	1,069	705	1,774	1,097	62%
1987	1,079	681	1,760	1,072	61%
1989	958	618	1,576	995	63%
1991	1,125	743	1,868	1,246	67%
1993	1,144	837	1,981	1,309	66%
1995	1,168	855	2,023	1,358	67%
1997	1,284	755	2,039	1,361	67%
1999	1,290	966	2,256	1,597	71%
2001	1,654	987	2,641	1,842	70%
2003	1,905	979	2,884	1,815	63%
2005	1,981	1,195	3,176	2,325	73%
2007	1,813	1,004	2,817	1,755	63%
2009	1,275	1,010	2,285	1,501	66%

Source: Arkansas Bureau of Legislative Research

Compensation

The Arkansas Constitution provides that members of the General Assembly should receive "such *per diem* pay and mileage for their services as fixed by law." (V, 16) Subsequent constitutional amendments (5, 15, 37, 48, 56, and 70) have specified the amount of salary to be paid to legislators.

Members of the House and of the Senate set the amount of the *per diem* payment, but they rely upon criteria established by the federal Internal Revenue Service. Legislators are also reimbursed for expenses, but these expenses must be documented.

Composition of the General Assembly

Even though being a member of the Arkansas General Assembly is not considered a full-time job, issues and committee assignments often require senators and representatives to spend much of their time on legislative matters. Occupations of General Assembly members vary greatly: agriculture; architecture; banking and investing; business and industry; education; funeral directing; health services; law; media and telecommunications; ministry; nonprofit organizations; and self-employment.

Term Limits

In 1992, the people of Arkansas successfully petitioned to place a term limits amendment on the ballot at the November general election. Amendment 73 provides a limit of two four-year terms for the state's constitutional officers and state senators. It provides a limit of three two-year terms for state representatives. These limits are some of the most restrictive in the country. The original language in Amendment 73 also attempted to limit terms for Arkansas' delegation in the U.S. Senate and U.S. House of Representatives. The U.S. Supreme Court, however, ruled these provisions unconstitutional.

Vacancies

Whenever a vacancy occurs in either house, the governor certifies in writing to the state committees of the recognized political parties the fact of the vacancy and asks the parties if they wish to hold primaries to determine their party's nominee. If, within 10 days, one or more parties reply affirmatively, the governor sets a deadline for filing and sets dates for the primary and for the special election. The primary must be held at least 30 and not more than 60 days after the deadline for filing, and at least ten days must be allowed for filing.

If neither party requests a primary, the governor issues a proclamation, which sets the deadline for filing and sets the date of the special election. Nominations may be made either upon certification by either the chairman or secretary of a convention of delegates of a political party or by petition of at least 100 electors in the district where the vacancy exists.

Independents may file nomination petitions signed by at least three percent of the qualified voters or by 10,000 qualified voters, whichever is less.

Legislative Procedures and Rules

The two primary procedures General Assembly members use to introduce legislation are resolutions and bills. Resolutions are expressions of legislative opinion or a means of expressing legislative intent, but they do not become law. One or both chambers may pass resolutions. A joint resolution is used to submit a proposed constitutional amendment to a vote of the people. All other resolutions requiring approval of both houses are sent to the governor for approval or disapproval. If disapproved by the governor, a resolution can be re-passed with a majority vote of both houses.

Any member of the Senate may introduce a bill or resolution by filing an original and 14 copies and 10 captions of the title with the secretary of the Senate. Senate bills are numbered 1 to 1,000. Any member of the House of Representatives may introduce a bill or resolution by filing an original and 14 copies and 10 captions of the title with the clerk of the House. House bills are numbered starting with 1,001. A legislator may propose a bill for a variety of reasons: personal interest, a request by a constituent or interest group, or a request by the governor or other constitutional officer. Bills recommended or endorsed by the governor are often called administration bills.

The process for a bill becoming a law is illustrated in the following table. When a bill is passed by both houses of the General Assembly and is signed by the governor, or if the governor neither approves nor vetoes a bill within 20 days of the General Assembly's adjournment, it becomes an act and is compiled in the Arkansas Code. An act goes into effect 90 days after the adjournment unless a bill contains a properly drawn emergency clause and, by a two-thirds vote, the General Assembly declares that an emergency exists. In such case, the measure becomes effective immediately.

How a Bill Becomes a Law in Arkansas

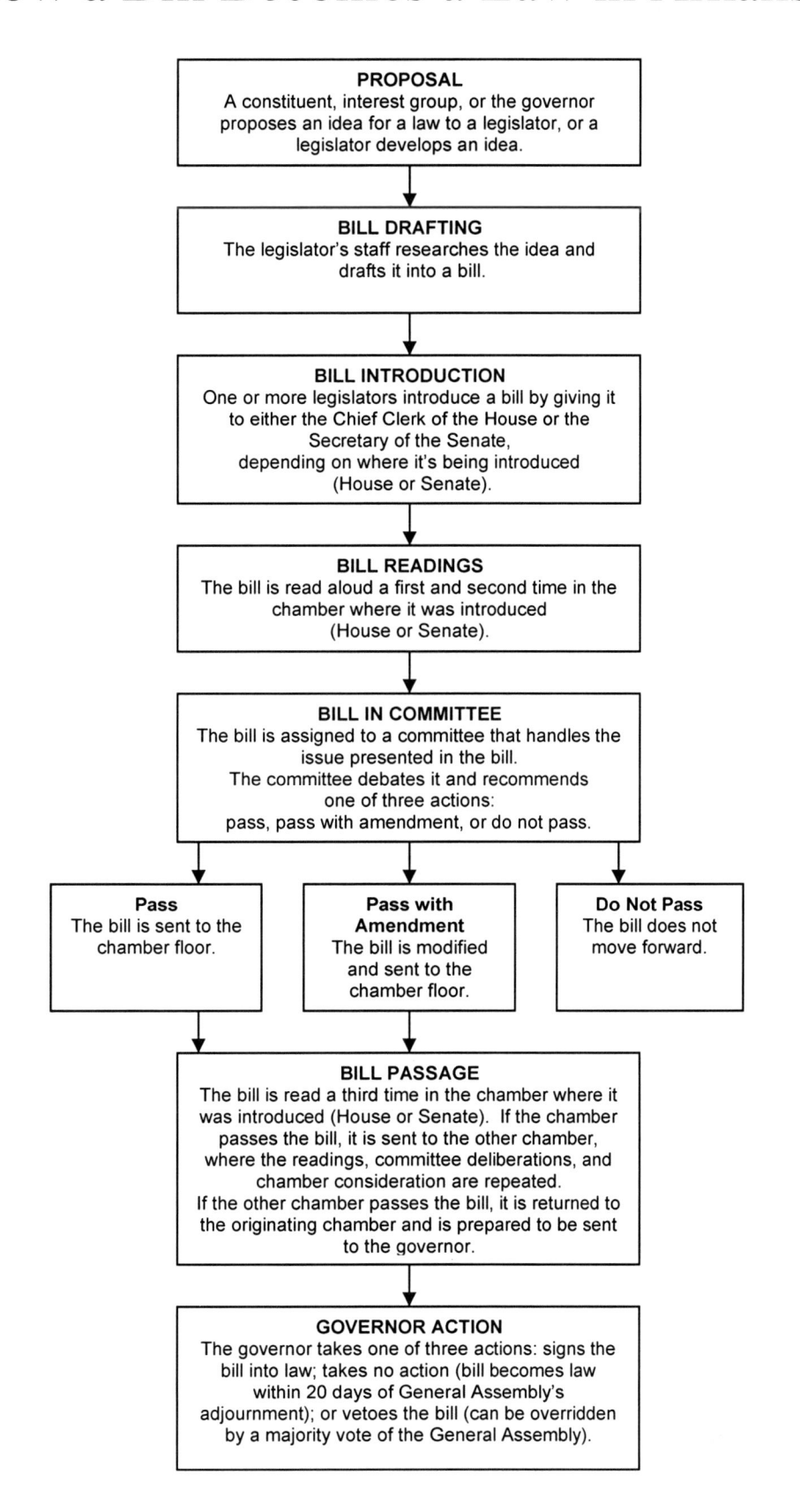

PROPOSAL
A constituent, interest group, or the governor proposes an idea for a law to a legislator, or a legislator develops an idea.

↓

BILL DRAFTING
The legislator's staff researches the idea and drafts it into a bill.

↓

BILL INTRODUCTION
One or more legislators introduce a bill by giving it to either the Chief Clerk of the House or the Secretary of the Senate, depending on where it's being introduced (House or Senate).

↓

BILL READINGS
The bill is read aloud a first and second time in the chamber where it was introduced (House or Senate).

↓

BILL IN COMMITTEE
The bill is assigned to a committee that handles the issue presented in the bill.
The committee debates it and recommends one of three actions:
pass, pass with amendment, or do not pass.

↓

Pass	**Pass with Amendment**	**Do Not Pass**
The bill is sent to the chamber floor.	The bill is modified and sent to the chamber floor.	The bill does not move forward.

↓

BILL PASSAGE
The bill is read a third time in the chamber where it was introduced (House or Senate). If the chamber passes the bill, it is sent to the other chamber, where the readings, committee deliberations, and chamber consideration are repeated.
If the other chamber passes the bill, it is returned to the originating chamber and is prepared to be sent to the governor.

↓

GOVERNOR ACTION
The governor takes one of three actions: signs the bill into law; takes no action (bill becomes law within 20 days of General Assembly's adjournment); or vetoes the bill (can be overridden by a majority vote of the General Assembly).

The legislative rules of procedure used in both houses are of two types: constitutional rules and chamber rules. The constitution declares "each house shall have the power to determine the rules of its proceedings" (V, 12), but it also specifies several rules that must be followed:

- majority of all members elected to each house shall constitute a quorum. (V, 11)

- "The sessions of each house and of committees of the whole shall be open unless when the business is such as ought to be kept secret." (V, 13)

- "Every bill shall be read at length on three different days in each house, unless the rules be suspended by two-thirds vote of the house..." (V, 22)

- "no bill shall become a law unless on its final passage the vote be taken by yeas and nays..." and a record of the vote be entered in the journal. (V, 22)

- no bill may be introduced in either house during the last three days of a session.

- no appropriation bill may be filed for introduction in either house later than the 50th day of the session except upon consent of two-thirds of the members elected to each house. (V, 34 and Joint Rule 16)

- no other bill may be introduced into either house later than the 50th day of the session except upon consent of two-thirds of the members elected to each house. (V, 34 and Joint Rule 16)

- a bill or any appropriation line item vetoed by the governor may be overridden by the legislature by a majority vote, even if the original measure required more than a majority vote. (VI, 15 and 17)

Other constitutional provisions regarding taxes and appropriations are listed in Chapter 10.

In addition to the rules prescribed by the constitution, there are also the rules of the Senate, rules of the House, and joint rules of the Senate and House. Enforcement of all rules is the responsibility of the presiding officer.

Rules of the Senate are developed by the Rules, Resolutions & Memorials Committee, consisting of fifteen members. All questions regarding Senate rules, joint rules, and order of business are referred to this Committee. The Senate is governed by the rules of parliamentary practice comprised in *Mason's Manual of Legislative Procedure* where applicable and not inconsistent with rules and orders of the Senate or joint rules of the Senate and the House. (Rule 24)

Rules of the House are drawn up by the Committee on Rules, which is composed of 15 members of the House and the parliamentarian, who serves *ex officio* and non-voting. House rules from the preceding General Assembly are automatically adopted as temporary rules for the next session. Permanent rules are adopted by majority vote, but may be changed only with a two-thirds vote (67 members). The House Committee on Rules has additional responsibilities since the speaker is charged with referring to it all matters dealing with alcohol, cigarettes, tobacco, tobacco products, coin operated amusement devices, vending machines, lobbying, pari-mutuel betting and similar legislation. Joint rules of the Senate and the House govern such items as joint sessions, operation of joint conference committees, transfer of bills between the two houses, engrossment and signing of bills.

Most rules of parliamentary procedure used in the Arkansas General Assembly are similar to those used in other legislative bodies, but there are several unusual or uncommon practices. For example, although the constitution requires that a bill be read three times on three different days, in practice only the title or even a portion of the title is read on the first and second readings. Further, since amendments can be made only when the bill is on second reading, if a bill should reach third reading, it must be returned to second reading to be amended. The third reading, which precedes the vote, may or may not be a reading in full.

Another distinctive procedure used by the Arkansas legislature is the clincher motion. The maker of this motion wishes to make reconsideration of a vote as difficult as possible. To accomplish this, the adoption of the clincher is moved, which is effectively two motions in one – a motion to reconsider and a motion to table the motion to reconsider. Since reconsideration has already been laid on the table, parliamentary rules state that any new motion to reconsider is out of order. The clincher requires a majority vote of all members. A procedure used for reconsideration of the measure that is used occasionally in the Senate and seldom in the House is a motion to expunge earlier action taken on any proceeding. It requires a two-thirds majority of the members elected.

Committee Organization

When the General Assembly is in session, its operation is often dependent upon the efficiency and effectiveness of its committees. Standing committees are the legislature's permanent committees that address mainstay issues. There are also select committees and special committees that deal with organizational and procedural matters. Joint committees facilitate collaboration between the two houses on essential matters of the state.

Standing Committees. In a major attempt to make the legislative process more effective, the standing committee structure of both houses was substantially changed in the early 1970's – by the House in 1971 and the Senate in 1973. Although membership of a few committees, such as the Joint Budget committee, is established by legislation, members of most Senate committees are selected by seniority, while the speaker according to House rules appoints most House committees.

Select Committees. Organization of the General Assembly is managed through the Senate and House select committees. The chamber-exclusive Senate select committees are the Rules, Resolutions & Memorials Committee, and the Efficiency Committee. The Joint committees are the Joint Budget Committee; Joint Committee on Public Retirement and Social Security Programs; Joint Committee on Energy; Joint Performance Review Committee; and Joint Committee on Advanced Communication and Information Technology. The chamber-exclusive select committees in the House are the House Management Committee and the House Rules Committee.

Joint Committees. During legislative sessions, the Joint Budget Committee is responsible for appropriation bills. Composed of members from both legislative chambers, the Joint Budget Committee prepares and introduces all appropriation bills for state agencies and institutions provided for under existing law. When an appropriation bill needs to be amended, the bill is automatically returned to the Joint Budget Committee for reconsideration.

There are other joint committees that operate during regular sessions and/or between sessions. The Joint Committee on Public Retirement and Social Security Programs reviews all bills involving retirement or social security programs of the state and of publicly supported agencies and institutions, and monitors their retirement systems. The Joint Committee on Energy makes continuing studies of energy resources and problems. These studies may be initiated by the committee or referred to it by the General Assembly. The Joint Performance Review Committee reviews state programs and agencies and conducts investigations into specific problem areas of the administration of state government. The Joint Committee on Advanced Communications and Information Technology is an effort by the state to address issues associated with changing communications and technological advances.

General Assembly Committees		
House	Senate	Joint
Advanced Communications and Information Technology	Agriculture, Forestry, and Economic Development	Academic Facilities Oversight
Aging, Children and Youth, Legislative and Military Affairs	Children and Youth	Advanced Communications and Information Technology
	City, County and Local Affairs	
Agriculture, Forestry, and Economic Development	Education	Arkansas State Game and Fish Commission Oversight
City, County and Local Affairs	Insurance and Commerce	
	Judiciary	Budget
Education	Public Health, Welfare, and Labor	Code Revision
House Management	Revenue and Taxation	Community Services Oversight and Planning Council
House Rules	Senate Rules, Resolutions, and Memorials	Economic and Tax Policy
Insurance and Commerce	State Agencies and Governmental Affairs	Educational Adequacy
Judiciary	Transportation, Technology, and Legislative Affairs	Educational Facilities
Public Health, Welfare, and Labor		Legislative Auditing
Public Transportation		Performance Review
Revenue and Taxation		Public Retirement and Social Security Programs
State Agencies and Governmental Affairs		Public School and School Motor Vehicle Insurance Advisory
		Rural Fire Departments Study

Source: Arkansas General Assembly

Interim Organization of the General Assembly

Between regular sessions of the General Assembly, the legislative branch of government continues to operate through the Legislative Council, the Legislative Joint Auditing Committee, and the Interim Subject Matter Committees. Also authorized to meet between sessions are the Rules Committees of the Senate and House and some joint committees.

Legislative Council. Although the Legislative Council is responsible for overseeing legislative organization and responsibilities between sessions, it does not have the power to enact legislation. Established by Act 264 of 1949, the Legislative Council's purpose is to collect data and information upon which legislative decisions will be made during regular sessions of the General Assembly. Although it cannot act on legislative matters, it may recommend specific policies and actions to the General Assembly and have bills drafted that include such recommendations.

Between sessions, the Legislative Council conducts pre-session budget hearings for all units of state government and then recommends to the General Assembly an itemized budget for all state departments, institutions, boards, commissions, and agencies. The Legislative Council is responsible for the coordination of the 10 joint subject matter interim committees that operate between sessions. In case of lawsuits involving the state of Arkansas, the Legislative Council determines whether the General Assembly has an interest in the litigation, and if so, determines the action necessary. In all its efforts the staff of the Bureau of Legislative Research assists the Legislative Council.

Interim Committees. Standing committees with similar subject matter that operate during sessions also serve as joint Senate and House committees between sessions. Membership is the same for the standing committees and the interim committees. Interim committees have oversight responsibilities in connection with state agencies operating in their subject matter fields. Such responsibilities involve agency investigations, performance evaluation, and expenditure review. The interim committees are also charged with making studies and investigations and determining the needs for appropriate legislation. The Bureau of Legislative Research does staff work for these studies. The committees are authorized to meet as often as necessary. However, if they find that they must meet more than twelve days a year, they must report to the Legislative Council, which will then determine whether funds are available to hold additional meetings.

Coordination of the committees' activities is the responsibility of the Legislative Council. Before an interim committee initiates a study, the Legislative Council must approve it so that there will be no duplication of efforts. When a member of the

General Assembly wishes to sponsor a proposal or resolution for study, the Legislative Council may refer it to one of the committees, in which case the member may serve *ex officio* as a member of the committee during the conduct of the study. Findings of the interim committees are advisory only and are not binding on the standing committees of the House or Senate. However, since the composition of the interim committees and the standing committees is the same, it is expected that the standing committees will act upon recommendations made by the interim committees when the General Assembly meets.

State agencies are instructed to "furnish the respective interim committees such information and assistance as the committees may reasonably request." (A.C.A. 10-3-213) Furthermore, each committee is responsible for receiving and reviewing any legislation suggested by the various agencies or by the governor.

Legislative Joint Auditing Committee. The purpose of the Legislative Joint Auditing Committee is to make sure that the money appropriated by the General Assembly is honestly and efficiently spent. The committee provides for the auditing of each department, institution, board, commission, office, and agency of the state government for the purpose of furnishing the General Assembly with information vital to the discharge of its constitutional duties. (A.C.A. 10-3-407) The committee is authorized to recommend to the General Assembly abolition or consolidation of any entity that it deems unnecessary based on its review of the agency's audit. The committee supervises the operation of the Division of Legislative Audit. The Division of Legislative Audit helps ensure proper accountability and stewardship of public funds and resources and provides relevant and vital information to the Legislative Joint Auditing Committee, the General Assembly, state agencies, political subdivisions, and the citizens of Arkansas.

Bureau of Legislative Research

Since legislators are part-time officials who do not have personal employees (unless hired at their own expense), the Bureau of Legislative Research performs staffing functions for all members of the General Assembly on a nonpartisan basis. The Bureau is under the direction of an executive director, who is selected by the Legislative Council, and who serves as the Council's secretary.

The Bureau researches issues for legislators, prepares legislation, and may provide advice concerning constitutional, statutory, and practical issues concerning the legislation. Specific service areas include:

- Research - subject research, legal research, budget and fiscal research, state personnel classification and compensation research, interim committee studies, revenue projections, and fiscal impact statements on proposed bills

- Drafting - preparation of bills (general bills and appropriation bills), resolutions, amendments to bills and resolutions, interim study proposals, and interim resolutions

- Committee Staffing – provides staff for all legislative committees and subcommittees, except the Legislative Audit Committee and its subcommittees and committees related to the internal operations of the House of Representatives or Senate

- Review of State Agency Rules - monitors rules as they are proposed by agencies to determine whether they comply with legislative intent and to ensure they are technically correct

- Codification of Laws - assists the Arkansas Code Revision Commission and works with the publisher of the Arkansas Code Annotated to compile and codify Acts of the General Assembly into the Arkansas Code Annotated

- Computer Services - maintains the computer system that serves the Senate, House of Representatives, and the Bureau of Legislative Research

Initiative and Referendum

According to Article 5, Section 1 of the state constitution, Arkansans have a direct voice in the legislative process. The first power reserved by the people is the initiative. Eight per cent of legal voters may propose any law, and 10% may propose a constitutional amendment by initiative petition. The second power reserved by the people is the referendum. Any number not less than six per cent of the legal voters may, by petition, call for a referendum vote against any general Act, any item of an appropriation bill, or any measure passed by the General Assembly. Support of the initiative and referendum has a long history in Arkansas. Even today it is the only southern state to have both the initiative and referendum processes available to the people. In the late nineteenth and early twentieth centuries, those active in the Populist movement gave support to the initiative and referendum, because they believed those devices would keep politics "pure." Labor, the Farmer's Union, and both the Republican and Democratic parties supported initiative and referendum.

George Donaghey included them in his platform in 1908, and it was the central issue of his 1910 campaign. A poorly drafted initiative and referendum constitutional amendment passed in 1910 by a 71% majority, but because of the poor wording and legal technicalities a second amendment was voted on in 1920. It passed and became Amendment 7.

The amendment states: "The people reserve to themselves the power to propose legislative measures, laws, and amendments to the Constitution, and to enact or reject the same at the polls independent of the General Assembly; and also reserve the power, at their own option, to approve or reject at the polls any entire act or any item of an appropriation bill."

Before any initiative or referendum petition is circulated, the sponsors must submit to the attorney general the original draft of the petition along with a proposed legislative or ballot title and popular name. The attorney general shall, within ten days, approve and certify or shall substitute and certify a more suitable and correct ballot title and popular name. If the attorney general fails to act or acts in a way unsatisfactory to the sponsors, they may appeal to the Supreme Court. On the other hand, if the attorney general determines that the ballot title is misleading or designed in a "manner that a vote 'for' the issue would be a vote against...and conversely...," the attorney general may reject the entire ballot title, popular name and petition, state his reasons for doing so, and instruct the petitioners to redesign the proposed measure and appropriate titles. (Act 209 of 1977)

Specifically, Amendment 7 states, "Eight per cent of the legal voters may propose any [state] law and ten percent may propose a constitutional amendment by initiative petition." In regard to the referendum on a state measure, Amendment 7 states that "any number not less than six per cent of the legal voters may, by petition, order the referendum against any general act, or any item of an appropriation bill, or measure passed by the General Assembly..." The total number of votes cast for the office of governor in the last preceding general election is the basis upon which the necessary number of signatures is computed. In addition to the percentage requirements, signatures must come from 15 or more counties and the percentage requirement from each of these counties must be equal to at least one half of the designated percentage (either six, eight, or ten, depending on the issue). Amendment 7 further states, "only legal voters shall be counted upon petitions." The responsibility for determining the legality of the petitioners and the sufficiency of the number of signatures is assigned to the secretary of state subject to review by the Arkansas Supreme Court. In ascertaining the sufficiency or insufficiency of the signatures on the petitions, all county clerks, unless granted a waiver from the State Board of Election Commissioners, must furnish "at cost" the secretary of state an alphabetical list of all registered voters in their respective counties.

Although the amendment states that only signatures of "legal voters" shall be counted, it is not specific about how a "legal voter" shall be identified, nor does it specify what information that "legal voter" needs to declare on the petition. In 1988, the signatures on numerous petitions were thrown out because they were illegible, were not identical with the signature the voter used when the voter registered to vote, or the precinct number was missing or incorrect. To clarify these questions, the 1989 General Assembly passed legislation that required all petitioners to print their name and declare their residence and the city or town where they live. However, "if a signature of a registered voter is sufficient to verify the voter's name, then it shall not be adjudged invalid for failure to sign the name, or write the residence and city or town of residence exactly as it appears on voter registration records, nor for failure to print the name in the space provided, all such information being an aid to verification rather than a mandatory requirement to perfect the validity of the signature." (Act 280 of 1989) Should the secretary of state determine that there is an insufficient number of legal signatures, the petitioners shall be given at least 30 more days in order to secure an adequate number of signatures.

State initiative petitions must be filed with the secretary of state at least four months before a general election. Referendum petitions must be filed with the secretary of state within 90 days after the final adjournment of the session at which an act was passed, "except when a recess or adjournment shall be taken temporarily for a longer period than 90 days, in which case such petition shall be filed not later than 90 days after such recess or temporary adjournment." (Amend. 7, Referendum)

After the secretary of state has ascertained that there are sufficient signatures, the secretary of state lets contracts for the publishing of the measure. At least six months before the election for constitutional amendments and eight weeks for other measures, all proposals must be published in at least one newspaper in each county for four consecutive weeks. Also the attorney general is required to prepare a concise abstract of the contents of every statewide initiative or referendum and give it to the secretary of state, who then sends copies to all county boards of election commissioners not less than 18 days before the election. At the same time, the secretary of state is required to send certified copies of the approved ballot titles and popular names for all statewide measures to all county boards of election commissioners.

The veto power of the governor cannot be used on any measure initiated by or referred to a vote of the people.

Other general provisions that apply to the initiative and referendum at all levels of government (state, county, and municipal) include:

- all initiative measures must be voted on at a regular (state, congressional, or municipal) election;

- referendum measures may be voted on at a special election called by the proper official;

- whenever a proper referendum petition has been filed, "such special election *shall* be called;"

- any measure submitted to the people becomes law when approved by a majority of those voting on the measure;

- there is no limit to the number of initiative or referendum measures that may be placed on the ballot for a vote of the people;

- "no law shall be passed to prohibit any person or persons from giving or receiving compensation for circulating petitions, nor to prohibit the circulation of petitions, nor in any manner interfere with the freedom of the people in procuring petitions but laws shall be enacted prohibiting and penalizing perjury, forgery, and all other felonies or other fraudulent practices in the securing of signatures or filing of petitions;" (Amend. 7, The Petition)

- "In the event of legal proceedings to prevent giving legal effect to any petition upon any grounds, the burden of proof shall be upon the person or persons attacking the validity of the petition." (Amend. 7, The Petition)

In recent years, the initiative process has become increasingly popular throughout the United States. In Arkansas, attempts to get initiated acts or amendments on the ballot have been consistently challenged. The challenges have included claims of misleading ballot titles; insufficient number, legibility and accuracy of signatures; and illegal certification of signatures by those passing the petitions.

Arkansans have seldom used the referendum, but the General Assembly frequently refers acts to the people for their approval. Despite the initiative and referendum "power of the people," the General Assembly still has the final say in initiative and referendum matters since, by a two-thirds vote, it can reverse the decision made by the people.

Initiative, Referendum, Referral and Recall in Arkansas

Provisions	State	County	Municipality
INITIATIVE			
Percentage of signatures necessary	Constitutional Amendment – 10% State Law – 8%	15%	15%
Percentage based on total number of votes cast in preceding election for	Governor	Circuit Clerk	Mayor or City Manager (highest vote cast for a director)
Qualifications of Petition Signers	Qualified electors of Arkansas	Qualified electors of county	Qualified electors of municipality
Petition filed with	Secretary of State	County Clerk	City Clerk
Deadline for filing	4 months before general election	60-90 days, exact number of days set by county	60-90 days, exact number of days set by municipality
REFERENDUM AND INITIATIVE			
Certification of Ballot Title and Popular Title submitted to	Attorney General	Attorney-at-Law licensed in Arkansas	Not Specified
Judge of legality and sufficiency of signatures	Secretary of State	County Clerk	City Clerk
Time allowed to judge legality and sufficiency of signatures	15 days	10 days	"without delay"
If inadequate number of signatures, time allowed to complete petition	30 days	At least 10 days	10 days
Subject to review by	Arkansas Supreme Court	Chancery Court	Chancery Court
Vote of people may be repealed or amended by	2/3 vote of General Assembly	2/3 vote of Quorum Court	2/3 vote of City Council or Board of Directors
REFERENDUM			
Percentage of signatures necessary	6 %	15%	15%
Percentage based on total number of votes cast in the preceding election for	Governor	Circuit Clerk	Mayor or City Manager (highest vote cast for a director)
Deadline for filing a petition	90 days after adjournment of General Assembly	Within 60 calendar days after passage and publication ordinance	30-60 days after passage of ordinance, exact number set by municipality
REFERRAL			
Referral of bill to vote of the people is permissible by	No Provision	3/5 vote of Quorum Court	2/3 vote of City Council or Board of Directors
RECALL			
Removal from office of elected official	No Provision	No Provision	In City Manager and City Administrator gov'ts, 35% of voters at last election to put on ballot; majority to remove

Comparison to Other States

In many ways the Arkansas legislature is similar to most other state legislatures. Arkansas is among 49 states that have a bicameral legislative structure. In addition, the primary legislative functions of making laws, appropriating money, overseeing the executive branch, and serving constituents are the major tasks for Arkansas state legislators. Another common feature of law-making bodies is that committees are the central mechanism for legislative action. Again, the Arkansas legislature follows this pattern by relying heavily upon committees to make policy. However, there are some areas where the Arkansas legislature is distinctive. Moreover, there are other substantive changes that are occurring in the legislative ranks.

A defining characteristic is term limits. Nineteen states have term limit laws. Currently, fourteen states have term limits in effect. As noted earlier, Arkansas has some of the most restrictive term limit rules. Some states only limit the number of consecutive terms in the legislature, but Arkansas' term limits are for a lifetime. Of course, most states have no term limits at all. There are some perceived benefits from term limits. It is believed term limits assist formerly under-represented groups in winning legislative seats. (Bowman and Kearney, 2002: 162; *The Book of the States*, 2008, p. 69)

Another unique feature of the Arkansas legislature is that it is composed of part-time legislators, which has a number of advantages. It is believed that part-time legislators better understand the needs and problems of average citizens. Moreover, these representatives have a realistic picture of how state government policies will impact people's lives. There are, however, some weaknesses with having a part-time legislature. Being part-time limits who can serve; very few people can leave a job for several months each year to work in the state legislature. Also, states must deal with increasingly complex economic and political problems that require more time from legislators. As state government expands its activities, greater legislative oversight is needed for executive actions.

Both part-time and full-time legislatures have their strengths and weaknesses. Historically, Arkansans have preferred a part-time or amateur legislature. A future challenge for the state and its citizens is balancing this historical preference for part-time officials with the political and economic challenges of the 21st century.

Additional Resources

Arkansas Bureau of Legislative Research
http://www.arkleg.state.ar.us/bureau/

Arkansas House of Representatives
http://www.arkansas.gov/house/

Arkansas General Assembly
http://www.arkleg.state.ar.us/assembly

Arkansas Senate
http://www.arkansas.gov/senate/

The National Conference of State Legislatures
http://www.ncsl.org

State Legislative Term Limits
http://www.termlimits.org

The Governor and Other Constitutional Officers

Chapter 3

In This Chapter

Governor

Lieutenant Governor

Attorney General

Secretary of State

Treasurer

Auditor

Land Commissioner

Terms to Know

clemency

constitutional officer

executive branch

pardon

veto

In contrast to the national government's single-executive structure, Arkansas has a plural executive structure. U.S. Presidents have the ability to appoint a cabinet of advisors, who then show some allegiance to them. Arkansas governors, on the other hand, must work within a plural executive setting with multiple elected executive officials. This structural feature divides executive branch power, meaning the governor does not control these officials. In fact, some of the governor's most visible political rivals may be other executive branch personnel.

Arkansas has seven constitutional officers, and all are chosen in statewide elections. The Arkansas Constitution provides for five specific constitutional officers: "The executive department of this State shall consist of a Governor, Secretary of State, Treasurer of State, Auditor of State and Attorney General, all of whom shall keep their offices in person at the seat of government and hold their offices for the term of two years (changed by Amendment 63) and until their successors are elected and qualified…" The Constitution also states the General Assembly may establish an office of Commissioner of State Lands. (VI, 1) The legislature took this step and created the position of Land Commissioner. In addition, the Arkansas Constitution was amended (Amendment 6) to create the position of Lieutenant Governor in 1926.

Governor

Qualifications and Length of Service. Most states and the United States government have very limited constitutional requirements for the chief executive, including age, citizenship, and residency. The Governor of Arkansas must be at least 30 years old, a U.S. citizen, and a resident of Arkansas for at least seven years. In contrast, the U.S. President must be at least 35 years old, a native-born U.S. citizen, and a U.S. resident for at least fourteen years. (*The Book of the States*, 2008: 185) It seems obvious that a large number of citizens meet the constitutional standard to hold executive office. However, the most important chief executive criteria are informal standards.

When evaluating an executive's length of service, it should be noted that historically turnover has been high in the office of governor. The two major factors contributing to this high turnover rate are constitutional limits and inadequate state resources. Arkansas has made policies over the last twenty years that have both encouraged and discouraged longer executive service. To increase executive tenure, the state legislature enacted Amendment 63, which altered the office terms for constitutional officers from two-year terms to four-year terms. However, the provisions of Amendment 73 restrict executive officers' tenure. The governor and all other Arkansas constitutional officers are limited to two four-year terms. This is clearly analogous to the term limits placed on the U.S. President in the 22nd Amendment. Presidents are limited to two four-year terms or ten years maximum service. These mandatory limits on length of service may hurt an executive official's ability to perform office functions. This is especially true for the chief executive position. When the governor is a "lame duck" and cannot seek office again, many resources are no longer available for political initiatives.

Preparation. Most states' governors have had prior public service experience. Over 30% of those elected governor previously held some other statewide office. Around 15% of successful gubernatorial candidates in the U.S. have served in the state legislature. Another 25 to 35% have served in Congress or some other public service area. (*The Book of the States*, 2008: 177) Arkansas' recent history seems to fit this selection pattern. Mike Beebe was a state senator and then served as attorney general. Both Mike Huckabee and his predecessor Jim Guy Tucker held the post of lieutenant governor before becoming governor. Former President Bill Clinton served as attorney general in his early political career, and former U.S. Senator David Pryor served three terms in the state legislature and three terms in the U.S. House of Representatives. Former U.S. Senator Dale Bumpers run unsuccessfully for the state legislature but served on the Charleston School Board.

Political Resources and Formal Powers. Chief executives in Arkansas have several resources to help achieve policy goals. Because the executive position is the major focus of the citizenry, there are increased opportunities for publicity. If the governor calls a press conference, media sources will be present to cover the event. In addition, chief executives have some appointment powers. The governor can select the Governor's Office staff and has the ability to appoint thousands of state citizens to over 300 boards and commissions.

Probably the most important resource available to the executive is bargaining and negotiation. Although legislators at the national and state level may introduce legislation, it is the governor's program that receives the most attention. One important power in the bargaining process is the executive's authority to prepare the budget. Although legislators may change and alter significant parts of any budget proposal, the executive sets the initial parameters that tend to frame the legislative debate. In addition, a governor gains some influence with legislators by giving support to legislators' funding priorities.

Another resource available to the governor when negotiating with the legislature is veto power. The governor's veto authority is somewhat limited, because the General Assembly can override it by a simple majority vote. This means that as long as the legislators who voted for the original bill are willing to cast the same vote, any gubernatorial veto can be overridden. In the case of appropriations bills, the governor has line-item veto power, whereby he can reject specific portions of legislative initiatives while signing the rest into law. In practice, Arkansas governors rarely exercise their veto power and instead rely upon other strategies to influence the legislature.

The governor can also call the General Assembly into special session. Historically, the power to call special sessions was an important gubernatorial resource. Now that Arkansas has annual legislative sessions, the need and likelihood for special sessions is reduced.

A final resource available to the governor is often referred to as the executive's judicial powers. The governor can grant pardons and commute sentences. Specifically, the pardoning powers of the governor are limited to the granting of "reprieves, commutations of sentence, and pardons after conviction" and "remitting of fines and forfeitures." (VI, 18)   If a governor pardons individuals who later commit other offenses, this can create political problems for the executive. Before 1993, the governor's authority to grant pardons and clemency was unconditional, but the legislature placed restrictions on this power by requiring that "at least thirty (30) days before granting an application for pardon, commutation of sentence, or remission of fine or forfeiture, the governor shall file with the secretary of state a notice of his intention to grant such an application." (A.C.A. 16-93-204)

Roles. The most common gubernatorial roles are: chief administrator, chief of state, chief legislator, military chief, chief of party, ultimate judge, and crisis manager. Many of the roles played by the executive are related to the formal powers and resources discussed earlier. The chief administrator role is most associated with the governor's leadership in the executive branch. The governor is responsible for the administration or implementation of many state programs. In addition, the governor appoints citizens to a wide range of state boards and commissions. Most importantly, the governor prepares the state budget.

The chief of state role focuses on the ceremonial functions of the gubernatorial office. The Arkansas governor represents the state in Washington, D.C., and in intergovernmental organizations like the National Governor's Association. This function may also be more important to the citizens of Arkansas. Arkansans tend view the governor in very personal terms. Therefore, when governors are performing these ceremonial functions, the citizenry believe they are developing the broader public's perception of the state.

The chief legislator role is linked to the governor's policy leadership. The legislative power of the governor is enhanced by the prestige of the office. Although legislators introduce a variety of bills, it is the "governor's program" that receives the most attention. The success of the governor's program depends upon the governor's ability to present the program early to members of the General Assembly and to the people, and then to use the office of governor to persuade the voters of the state of the value of certain legislation. This is important because legislators frequently maintain that they feel they must vote according to the wishes of their constituents. If those constituents inform them that they favor the governor's program, it stands a good chance of passing. In addition, the governor delivers an annual "State of the State" message to help set legislative priorities.

Other roles played by the governor are military chief and chief of party. As military chief, the governor is able to call out the Army National Guard to keep order and peace during natural disasters and civil disturbances. The chief of party role is unique in the Arkansas context. The governor is usually the most prominent party leader in two-party states. Traditionally, Arkansas has not been seen as a two-party state, because Democrats have held the majority in the state legislature since the end of Reconstruction. This partisan divide seems to be slowly changing as more Republicans are elected to the state legislature. Moreover, Arkansas governors can appoint citizens from their party to boards and commissions. In addition, they can provide a training ground for fellow partisans to work in the executive branch and gain valuable political experience. The chief of party role can assist in efforts to build a grassroots party organization. However, some analysts argue that party chief role power has declined over the last few decades. (Muchmore and Beyle, 1983: 50-51)

The ultimate judge role is related to the governor's judicial powers. As noted earlier, the governor has the authority to pardon criminals and commute their sentences. Also, the governor can grant stays of execution in capital punishment cases. It is the executive's power to deal with these life and death situations that is most associated with the ultimate judge role. Governors have other tasks to perform in the criminal justice system. Individuals who commit state crimes must be tried in the state where the crime occurred. If they flee the state, they must be returned for trial. It is the governor who has the power of extradition in response to a request from another state for the return of a fugitive. In addition, the governor has the power to fill vacancies in the judiciary. However, there is a major limitation to this appointment power. The constitution prevents those appointed from running for that office when their appointed term ends. However, these individuals can use this experience to assist them in the electoral pursuit of other judgeships.

The governor also functions as a crisis manager. When problems arise, the citizenry believe the governor will respond to these situations. When natural disasters occur or other crises erupt, the governor is expected to organize the state response and address these problems. This role can be an asset to a governor when the public believes the executive has handled a crisis effectively. However, this role can also lead to problems for the governor. If citizens feel the governor's response is not productive, it can lead to public displeasure and declining political support.

Generally, there is a close relationship between the governor and the people in Arkansas. Many citizens consider it their right to ask the governor to solve any personal difficulties they might have. As a result, the governor's staff spends considerable time on casework and "walking through the system" with a citizen. Such casework may involve life and death situations, health or human service problems, educational difficulties, environmental conditions, or other situations. This personal connection may be stronger in Arkansas than in other more heavily populated states. In addition, it can be a political asset when the governor seeks legislative approval for policy initiatives.

Lieutenant Governor

The office of lieutenant governor exists in 43 states. As noted earlier, Arkansas' lieutenant governor position was re-created by constitutional amendment in 1926, having briefly existed in the 1868 Arkansas Constitution. Qualifications for lieutenant governor are the same as those for governor: United States citizen, at least 30 years of age, and resident of Arkansas for seven years or more. The tasks and responsibilities of Arkansas' lieutenant governor are very similar to counterparts in other states. The lieutenant governor serves as president of the Senate. In this capacity, the lieutenant governor can cast tie-breaking votes on state Senate legislation. Twenty-six lieutenant governors have this authority. In addition, if the governor is removed from office, dies, is unable to discharge the powers and duties of the office, resigns, or is absent from the state, the lieutenant governor usually assumes the duties and powers of the office of governor. However, the movement of Arkansas' lieutenant governor to the governor's office was not always so clear. Following the election of Governor Bill Clinton to the presidency, there was considerable debate about the succession of Lieutenant Governor Jim Guy Tucker to the governorship. Amendment 6 states that the powers and duties of governor "shall devolve upon the lieutenant governor for the residue of the term," but it does not specifically state that the lieutenant governor shall *become* the governor, receive the salary designated for the governor, live in the Governor's Mansion, or be eligible for such other privileges as are assigned to the governor. The issue was appealed to the Arkansas Supreme Court which ruled in *Bryant vs. English*, 311 Ark. 187 [1992] that "the Office of Governor itself devolves upon the Lieutenant Governor."

There are some distinctive features of Arkansas' lieutenant governorship. Twenty-four states select the governor and lieutenant governor as a team. Similar to the selection of U.S. President and Vice-President, this step is taken to avoid partisan conflict between two executive offices. However, Arkansas selects the governor and lieutenant governor in separate elections. This feature can be important due to another characteristic of Arkansas governance. If for any reason the governor is absent from the state, the lieutenant governor becomes the acting governor. While the governor is out of state, the lieutenant governor could commute criminals' sentences or exercise any other gubernatorial legal power. Many analysts believe this policy should be changed in an era of modern communication. The legislature attempted to address this problem with an amendment to overhaul the executive branch in 2002. However, the Arkansas electorate defeated this proposal.

One final distinguishing element of Arkansas' lieutenant governor is that it is the only constitutional office that is considered a part-time position. As a result, the lieutenant governor's annual salary is the lowest of all the constitutional officers. This part-time status also affects the lieutenant governor's office budget and staff support. (Act 3 of 2003)

Secretary of State

The secretary of state position exists in all fifty states except Hawaii. It is an elected office in 36 states. The Arkansas Constitution declares that the secretary of state "shall keep a full and accurate record of all the official acts and proceedings of the Governor..." (VI, 21) At present, the secretary of state is not only custodian of all the official acts and proceedings of the governor, but also the official records of the General Assembly, including the Legislative Journals and the original copies of all acts of the General Assembly. The office of the secretary of state maintains a list of all Arkansas boards and commissions to which the governor makes appointments. It keeps the records on incorporations and annexations, corporate charters, notary public commissions, corporate franchise taxes, trademarks and service marks, and federal tax liens. It is the office for registration of lobbyists' expenditures, charitable organizations, professional fundraisers, machine guns, home builders, financial interest filings and Uniform Commercial Code (UCC) filings. Election responsibilities include receiving political practice pledges and campaign expenditure accounts of candidates for public office, determining the sufficiency of legal signatures on initiative and referendum petitions, publishing amendments, and canvassing and announcing election returns.

The secretary of state is also the legal custodian of the State Capitol building, the capitol grounds, and the furniture and fixtures of the State Capitol, and is in charge of the State Capitol Police Department. The secretary of state, the governor, and the attorney general compose the State Board of Apportionment, which is responsible for establishing legislative district boundaries following each federal census. In addition, the secretary of state deals with the voting process throughout the state and certifies candidates, ballot issues, and elections.

Most of these functions are also the major tasks of secretary of state offices throughout the United States. Primarily, the office focuses on important record keeping and clerical activities. (*The Book of the States,* 2008: 201-217)

Attorney General

Currently, 43 states utilize the attorney general office. Arkansas' attorney general serves as the state's chief legal counsel. The attorney general represents all but two state agencies and most of the various state boards and commissions in this capacity. In addition, the office provides non-binding legal opinions to state officials. These opinions may not be legally binding, but other public officials are usually reluctant to oppose these rulings. With the governor and the secretary of state, the attorney general serves on the State Board of Apportionment, which is responsible for establishing legislative district boundaries following each federal census. The attorney general's office is divided into six departments: Civil, Community Relations, Criminal, Medicaid, Opinions, and Public Protection. Because of efforts in consumer protection, Medicaid fraud, and other citizen-friendly tasks, the attorney general tends to have a positive public image.

Arkansas' attorney general is responsible for many of the same tasks as other state attorney generals. In fact, there has been a growing cooperation among the various states' attorney general offices. One example of this cooperation is a major tobacco lawsuit. Several state attorneys general, including Arkansas, won a $200 billion settlement for reimbursements for state Medicaid-related health care expenses. It appears the offices operate in very similar fashions. (*The Book of the States,* 2008: 222)

The office of attorney general can be a stepping-stone toward higher political office. Examples of those who served as attorney general in their early political careers include Bill Clinton, Mark Pryor, and Mike Beebe.

Treasurer

Thirty-seven states have an elected state treasurer. The treasurer's duties include receiving and keeping all the monies of the state not expressly required by law to be kept by some other person; disbursing the public money by warrants drawn upon the treasury; and keeping a just, true and comprehensive account of all monies received and disbursed. Basically, the treasurer functions as a bank for the state government.

The treasurer's office is organized by the services it provides. The Local Government Services section is responsible for distributions to Arkansas counties. These distributions are county and municipal aid (turnback) and local sales and use taxes. The Cash Management division works with banks, investment firms, and the Department of Finance and Administration, initiating daily payment wires and funds transfers. The division also distributes general and special state revenues on a monthly basis to state agencies, colleges, and universities. Balancing the state's general ledger is another duty of the Cash Management division. The treasurer's office is also responsible for the state's Money Management Trust Fund, which was established to be used by state agencies and local governments as a vehicle for enhancing investment opportunities and earnings for idle cash. Another investment service of the treasurer's office is the CD Trusts Investments program, which allows state agencies to invest their trust funds in certificates of deposit with Arkansas banks. The Receipts Processing department receives, verifies, and documents deposits on a daily basis. The Warrants Processing department administers warrants (checks) written by various state agencies for services rendered to them. The Collateral area of the treasurer's office ensures that state treasury funds deposited with a financial institution are secured at all times by conveyance of a perfected security interest in eligible securities as prescribed by Arkansas law.

In addition to carrying out the state's primary financial management duties, the treasurer serves on the State Board of Finance and on the boards of the Arkansas Public Employees Retirement System (APERS), the Arkansas Teacher Retirement System, and the Arkansas State Highway Employees Retirement System (ATRS). The tasks of Arkansas' treasurer are very much like those in other states. (*The Book of the States,* 2008: 228)

Auditor

The auditor is an elected position in 25 states. A very similar position called a comptroller is elected in 13 states. The auditor is the general accountant of the state, serves as disbursing agent for federal grant funds, and keeps public vouchers, books, documents, and papers relating to state debt, reserves and other fiscal matters. The auditor also inspects voter registration affidavits and assists county clerks in their capacity as voter registrars. In addition, the auditor serves on the Boards of Continuing Education for county and circuit clerks, county treasurers and county collectors.

The auditor is also responsible for providing the efficient and orderly transfer of abandoned property to the state and sponsors the annual "Great Arkansas Treasure Hunt." The primary goal of the treasure hunt is to reunite Arkansans with funds that are rightfully theirs. The auditor also serves on the State Board of Finance and is an *ex officio* board member of the Public Employees Retirement System (PERS) and the State Teachers Retirement System.

Land Commissioner

When compared to other states, the commissioner of state lands is Arkansas' most unique constitutional office. Only five states have an elected land commissioner. The primary responsibility of Arkansas' land commissioner is to oversee the disposition of tax delinquent property. These lands may either be redeemed by their owners, or if not redeemed within the statutory time frame, sold by the commissioner's office at public sale. Whether the property is redeemed or sold, the total amount of tax money and interest collected on delinquent property is returned to the county where the property is located.

The land commissioner's office is divided into two departments. The Records Division processes payment of delinquent property taxes, processes requests for patent information, and houses county land certification records. The Sales Division researches tax delinquent land titles to notify owners and interested parties that land has been scheduled for sale. The division also conducts public auctions of tax delinquent property and processes purchase offers on negotiated sales.

The land commissioner is empowered to donate tax delinquent lots for urban homesteading within cities and towns and to donate tax delinquent properties to state agencies, Arkansas supported colleges and universities, and local governmental units, when the donation of such properties is in the best interest of the state. In addition, the land commissioner is responsible for the competitive bidding and the leasing of all mineral interests on state owned lands. By law, the land commissioner also maintains the deeds for all property owned by the state or its agencies and institutions with the exception of the Arkansas Highway and Transportation Department. Moreover, the office houses the original patent records of the state. Also, copies of State Land Office land plats are maintained in the commissioner's office along with the corresponding field survey notes.

Additional Resources

Arkansas Constitutional Officers
http://www.arkansas.gov/government_exec.php

Council of State Governments
http://www.csg.org

National Governors Association
http://www.nga.org

The State Bureaucracy

Chapter 4

State bureaucratic personnel play a pivotal role in the implementation and delivery of essential governmental services. As a percentage of the U.S. population, the number of federal government employees has declined over the last two decades. The number of state workers, on the other hand, has increased during this time period. The primary explanation for this phenomenon is the federal government relies upon state employees to carry out national programs. (Bowman and Kearney, 2002: 208-9) Therefore, the importance of state bureaucratic personnel cannot be underestimated.

State Personnel Management

One unique feature of Arkansas' state employment policy is the lack of a merit system or a system whereby state employees are promoted and rewarded solely on the basis of ability. This distinction exists due to state right-to-work employment provisions. States that enforce right-to-work statutes prohibit trade unions and employees from making membership or union dues a condition of employment. Federal anti-discrimination statutes, however, place some limits on state employment practices. That is, Arkansas is not free to discriminate because of race, color, religion, sex, age, or national origin. However, the job security provided in the federal civil service is not available to most state employees.

The Office of Personnel Management (OPM), an office in the Department of Finance and Administration, bears the primary responsibility for administering the state's personnel system. OPM has four sections: (1) classification and compensation – classifying and evaluating jobs, collecting salary data, and providing personnel management services; (2) payroll – creating and maintaining human resources data for the state's central accounting system; (3) inter-agency training programs; and (4) research and technical services – providing information, analyses, and advice on personnel related rules and regulations. Therefore, the efforts of the OPM to classify, compensate, and train state employees is essential to the success of governmental programs.

In This Chapter

State Personnel Management

Major State Agencies

Boards and Commissions

Comparison to Other States

Terms to Know

general revenue

merit system

special revenue

Organizational Structure and Reorganization Efforts

Administration of government in Arkansas is constantly being organized and reorganized depending on actions by the General Assembly and by the presiding governor. However, most of these changes tend to involve a few agencies at a time. The state bureaucracy has not experienced a major overhaul in over three decades. The last dramatic state government reorganization occurred in 1971 under Governor Dale Bumpers. This reorganization plan consolidated over 60 state agencies into thirteen major state departments. In addition, the directors of these departments then served as Governor Bumpers' cabinet. Since that time new departments have been added and other departments have been eliminated and the cabinet system has varied with each new chief executive.

In general, dramatic changes in state government structure are rare. This is understandable since many political participants do not desire reorganization because they have access and influence under the current structure. Legislators, interest group representatives, and average citizens may have established ties and contacts that would be eliminated with reorganization. Moreover, previous reorganization successes did not solve some of the most pressing state government concerns.

Major State Agencies

Agriculture. The Arkansas Agriculture Department provides information and research services related to state agricultural interests. It is comprised of the Forestry Commission, Livestock and Poultry Commission, State Plant Board, and Aquaculture Division.

Arkansas Building Authority. The Arkansas Building Authority, formerly known as Arkansas State Building Services, was created in 1975. The ABA is guided and governed by the Arkansas Building Authority Council. The ABA Council consists of 11 members whose duties are to set policies, guidelines, standards and procedures, which ABA personnel implement. The ABA is authorized to obtain sites; to construct, equip, maintain and operate public buildings; to authorize the leasing of property for and by state agencies; to assist state agencies in architectural and engineering needs; and to assist other state agencies in the construction and maintenance of public buildings. Records regarding most of these transactions are kept and maintained by the ABA. The ABA also maintains a database of state owned property, leasing transactions, and on-going capital improvement projects. The ABA includes the following sections: Design Review, Construction, and Real Estate Services.

Arkansas Heritage. Since 1975, the Department of Arkansas Heritage has promoted and coordinated the discovery, preservation, and presentation of Arkansas' natural and cultural resources. In addition to its central administrative office, the department includes the Arkansas Arts Council, Commemorative Commission, Historic Arkansas Museum Commission, Natural Heritage Commission, Old State House Commission, Delta Cultural Center, Natural & Cultural Resources Council, and the Mosaic Templars Cultural Center.

Arkansas State Police. Formed in 1935, the Arkansas State Police Department enforces motor vehicle laws, traffic laws, and other state laws relating to the protection of motorists on state highways. It also enforces criminal laws and apprehends offenders. Members of the department are conservators of the peace and as such have the powers possessed by policemen in cities and sheriffs in counties, except that the Arkansas State Police may exercise such powers anywhere in the state. The department includes the Administrative Services Division, Highway Patrol Division, Criminal Investigation Division, Crimes Against Children Division, and Highway Safety Office.

Correction. The Department of Correction was created in 1968 and is under the authority of the Arkansas Board of Correction and Community Punishment. Department responsibilities include assuming custody, control and management of the state penitentiary; executing the orders of Arkansas criminal courts; and providing for the custody, treatment, rehabilitation, and restoration of adult offenders. Along with its central administrative office in Pine Bluff, the Department of Correction consists of the following facilities: Benton Unit; Boot Camp Program at Wrightsville; Cummins Unit at Grady; Delta Regional Unit at Dermott; Diagnostic Unit at Pine Bluff; East Arkansas Regional Unit at Brickeys; Grimes Unit at Newport; Hawkins Center for Women at Wrightsville; Maximum Security Unit at Tucker; McPherson Unit at Newport; Mississippi County Work Release Center at Luxora; North Central Unit at Calico Rock; Northwest Arkansas Work Release Center at Springdale; Ouachita River Unit at Malvern; Pine Bluff Unit; Randall L. Williams Correctional Facility at Pine Bluff; Texarkana Regional Correction Center; Tucker Unit at Pine Bluff; Varner Unit at Grady; and Wrightsville Unit.

Economic Development Commission. Since 1955, the Economic Development Commission has led statewide economic development efforts, advanced job creation strategies, promoted communities, and supported the training and growth of a skilled workforce. The commission consists of 16 members appointed to four-year terms by the governor. These appointments are made with the advice and consent of the state senate. At least three members are from each of the four congressional districts and four members are appointed at large.

Education. Established in 1867, the Department of Education is responsible for implementing all state statutes dealing with public education (except higher education); the accreditation of schools; the administration of federal educational and school related programs; the providing of textbooks and instructional materials, supervisors and specialists; and the direction of vocational, technical and adult education programs. The department is directed by the State Board of Education, which is the policy making body for public elementary and secondary education in Arkansas. The board is composed of nine individuals appointed by the governor. Two members are selected from each of the state's four congressional districts and one member is selected at large. Members are appointed to seven-year terms. The Department of Education has five divisions: Academic Accountability; Fiscal and Administrative Services; Human Resources; Learning Services; and Research and Technology.

Environmental Quality. The Department of Environmental Quality is the umbrella organization for regulatory activities that seek to protect the state's environment. The department has six regulatory divisions that focus on specific elements of the environment: air, hazardous waste, regulated storage tanks, solid waste, mining, and water. The department also has four environmental assistance divisions that offer support to citizens, communities, and regulated businesses: Emergency Response; Environmental Preservation & Technical Services; Legal; and Public Outreach and Assistance. Administrative sections take care of the department's fiscal, management, and computer service needs.

Finance and Administration. The Department of Finance and Administration (DFA) provides assistance to all state agencies in the management of their appropriated funds, personnel and property, while exercising statutory controls over the agencies in these areas. The director of the DFA is the chief fiscal officer of the state. Moreover, the director provides budget projections which guide state funding decisions. DFA also collects the general and special revenues assessed by law and registers all motor vehicles and drivers. In addition, DFA administers and enforces the law governing the sale and consumption of all alcoholic beverages and administers pari-mutuel horse and dog racing regulations. The department is organized into two major divisions and various independent offices: Division of Management Services, which includes the Offices of Accounting, Budget, Employee Benefits, Intergovernmental Services, Personnel Management, and Procurement; and Division of Revenue, which includes the Offices of Child Support Enforcement , Driver Services, Excise Tax

Administration, Field Audit, Income Tax Administration, Motor Vehicles, Revenue Legal Services, and State Revenue Office Administration. The independent offices are Administrative Services, Information Services, Alcoholic Beverage Control Administration, Alcoholic Beverage Control Enforcement, Criminal Detention Facilities Review, and Racing Commission.

Game and Fish. Created in 1945, the Game and Fish Commission oversees the protection, conservation and preservation of various species of fish and wildlife in Arkansas. This is done through habitat management, fish stocking, hunting and fishing regulations, and a host of other programs conducive to helping Arkansas' wildlife flourish. The commission also generates public awareness of wildlife management through education programs, hunting and fishing regulations, and environmental efforts. The commission consists of seven Arkansans appointed by the governor to seven-year terms. An eighth, non-voting, member sits as chair of the University of Arkansas at Fayetteville's Department of Biology.

Health. The Department of Health provides statewide services for wide range of public health needs. In addition to its administrative office in Little Rock, the department staffs public health units in each of Arkansas' 75 counties. Its Vital Records section maintains and issues official copies of birth, death, marriage, and divorce certificates. The department also issues permits and occupational licenses and certification for health-related professions and occupations that affect public health. The department carries out regulations and policies put forth by the State Board of Health.

Higher Education. Established in 1971, the Department of Higher Education serves as the administrative staff for the Arkansas Higher Education Coordinating Board. The board consists of 12 members who are appointed by the governor and serve staggered six-year terms. As part of its responsibilities, the staff develops and implements board policies and procedures. Additionally, the department reviews and approves academic programs; administers statewide financial aid programs and contracts with the Southern Regional Education Board for support of graduate and first professional study outside of Arkansas; recommends institutional operating, capital, and personal services budgets; and collects and reports on student and course data as part of a statewide data base and academic program inventory for policy studies.

Highway and Transportation. The Department of Highway and Transportation was established in 1977 and is responsible for coordinating public and private transportation activities and implementing a safe and efficient intermodal transportation system. In addition to its central administrative office in Little Rock, the department has 10 district headquarters, 85 county area maintenance headquarters, and 31 resident engineer offices throughout the state. The department is governed by the State Highway Commission, composed of five members serving 10-year terms and appointed by the governor with the advice and consent of the Arkansas Senate.

Human Services. Created in 1971, the Arkansas Department of Human Services (DHS) is the largest state agency with more than 7,500 employees working in all 75 counties. Every county has at least one local office where citizens can apply for any of the services the department offers. In addition to its administrative offices, DHS has 10 major divisions: Aging and Adult Services; Behavioral Health Services; Child Care; Child and Family Services; County Operations; Developmental Disabilities Services; Medical Services; Services for the Blind; Volunteerism; and Youth Services.

Information Systems. Established in 1997, the Department of Information Systems provides a variety of information technology guidelines and services to state entities, including support for software, hardware, data storage, network, and telecommunications applications.

Labor. Since 1913, the responsibility for administering and enforcing Arkansas' labor laws has rested with the Arkansas Department of Labor. Some of its responsibilities include the collection of unpaid wages for employees, the issuance of work permits, and the enforcement of child labor, minimum wage, overtime, prevailing wage, and private employment agency laws. The department's divisions include Labor Standards, Mediation and Conciliation, Occupational Safety and Health, and Occupational Licensing and Code Enforcement.

Parks and Tourism. In 1971, the General Assembly enacted a law that changed the Publicity and Parks Commission, which had been in existence since 1955, to the Department of Parks and Tourism. The State Parks, Recreation and Travel Commission, is composed of 13 members appointed by the governor plus one commissioner emeritus, sets policy for the department

The Parks Division operates 52 parks and museums, offers technical assistance programs for cities and counties in regard to parks and museums, and administers grants-in-aid programs for museums and outdoor recreation. The Tourism Division administers Arkansas' advertising and promotional programs, including supervision of the Tourism Development Trust Fund. Act 38 of 1989 with the levying of a 2% gross receipts tax created this fund. The tax is on tourist-related business, and the funds collected must be used exclusively for promotion of tourism in Arkansas. Moreover, Amendment 75, which increased the state sales tax by one-eighth of a cent, provides additional revenue for the Department of Parks and Tourism. This division also operates a number of tourist information centers throughout the state.

Another important unit within the Parks and Tourism Department is the History Commission. Created by the General Assembly in 1905, it is responsible for the state archives and for collecting and preserving the source materials of the history of Arkansas. The commission consists of seven members appointed by the governor to seven-year terms. The state historian directs the commission staff. In 1991, the Black History Commission was created to collect black historical materials for the Arkansas History Commission; to encourage research in Arkansas black history; and to cooperate with the Arkansas Department of Education in the development of African American historical materials for use in public schools.

In 1975, the General Assembly added the Great River Road Division to the Department of Parks and Tourism. Its policy board is the Arkansas Mississippi River Parkway Commission, composed of one member from each of the ten counties bordering the Mississippi River plus one commissioner emeritus. The Great River Road Division is charged with promoting all aspects of the ten counties, and also working with the other states of the International Mississippi River Parkway Commission to secure funding for the development and promotion of the road.

Workforce Education. The Department of Workforce Education oversees career and technical education programs, adult and youth apprenticeship programs, and adult education programs. In addition to its administrative support personnel, the department is comprised of three divisions: Adult Education, Career and Technical Education, and Arkansas Rehabilitation Services.

Workforce Services. Formerly known as the Employment Security Division, the Department of Workforce Services operates through a central administrative office and is responsible for operating the local employment offices throughout the state. The department is divided into three areas: Employment Services, Unemployment Insurance, and Labor Market Information.

Boards and Commissions

Over 3,000 Arkansas citizens serve on state boards and commissions. Some are volunteers who pay their own expenses, some have their expenses paid, and others receive compensation for their services. Boards and commissions vary in size from three to 38 members, but most consist of five to nine members. In general, the larger ones are advisory and the smaller ones have administrative, regulatory, or quasi-judicial responsibilities. Terms of members range from two to ten years, though most have terms of four, five, or six years. All members serve, even though their terms may have expired, until a replacement is appointed. Most members of boards and commissions serve by appointment of the governor with the Arkansas Senate's approval. Although in some states, terms of boards and commission members end with the completion of the governor's term, in Arkansas, terms are staggered and members complete their term of office, no matter who is governor. Many appointed by the governor must be chosen from lists supplied by the General Assembly, by various departments, or by either public or private professional organizations. Other members serve *ex officio* by virtue of a position they already hold, and a few are appointed by someone other than the governor.

State law requires attendance of members at board or commission meetings, and any member missing three successive regular meetings is subject to removal. Members may be removed for "good cause" such as "conduct constituting a criminal offense involving moral turpitude, gross dereliction of duty, or gross abuse of authority." (Act 160 of 1979) They may also be removed for participating in an illegal closed meeting subject to the Freedom of Information laws.

State boards and commissions oversee the expenditures of between 25% and 30% of all state revenues. This is exclusive of public education funds, but does include funds administered by the Highway Commission and Game and Fish Commission and by the boards of trustees of institutions of higher education. The financial functions of a board or commission may involve review of budgets that vary in size. Duties may extend to investment responsibilities for large sums of money—bonds, pension funds, and tax reserves. Some boards are authorized to distribute federal and state grant monies. Some may not be responsible for direct expenditures of funds, but their decisions may have an impact on how money is spent by citizens or the state. The licensure boards are responsible not only for determining how their fees shall be spent but also for collecting them.

The funds for which boards and commissions are responsible come primarily from three main sources: general revenues, special revenues, and cash funds. General revenues come primarily from state taxes, including income taxes, sales and use taxes, severance taxes and taxes on alcohol, tobacco, and racing. Special revenues are those collected for specific purposes and may not be transferred to general revenues, such as fees and license money collected by the Highway and Transportation Department and the Game and Fish Commission. Cash funds come primarily from fees charged by licensing boards and commissions for examinations, permits, and licenses.

Regardless of their financial responsibilities or the source of funds, no board or commission can expend monies without an appropriation by the General Assembly.

The process for getting budget approval is the same as for any state official or department. Licensure boards and commissions play an especially important role in the regulation of the occupations of Arkansas citizens. The licensing process is concerned primarily with the licensing, certification, or registration of practitioners, but it also may involve the licensing of businesses and places of business. A licensed practitioner is one who has passed appropriate examinations and met all standards imposed by the Arkansas board, commission or agency involved. A certified practitioner is one who has met pre-determined standards, and a registered practitioner is one who has simply filed name, address and qualifications with the board or commission before practicing. Most licensure boards also provide regulatory services by monitoring those they have licensed to be sure they are practicing according to appropriate standards and by hearing complaints from citizens who feel they have been wronged. Boards may also take disciplinary action against operators not practicing according to standards. Such action ranges from reprimands to fines, suspension, or revocation of license.

The principle of separation of powers maintains that the legislative body passes laws that set policy and the executive enforces those laws, and boards and commissions are generally considered part of the executive branch. However, it is seldom as simple as that since the fine line between checking to be sure that legislative intent is being implemented correctly and interference is often difficult to determine. Oversight of boards and commissions by the Arkansas legislature involves review of budgets, contracts, procedural rules of operation and administrative rules and orders, and financial audits. The first three tasks are performed by the Legislative Council and the fourth by the Legislative Joint Auditing Committee. In 1988, the Game and Fish Commission brought suit against the Legislative Council, charging that review of contracts by the Review and Advice Subcommittee of the Legislative Council was unconstitutional in that it violated the separation of powers doctrine. The Arkansas Supreme Court decided in favor of the Game and Fish Commission, stating that "the executive authority should be free, not only from blatant usurpation of its powers, but from paralyzing interference as well." The court's ruling reduced the Legislative Council's "review and advice" function to simply "review," but since the legislature is still responsible for appropriating all expenditures of the state departments and agencies, the issue of oversight vs. interference continues to exist.

There have also been attempts to require performance or management audits and to consolidate or eliminate many of the boards and commissions, but such attempts have had varying degrees of success. In 1977 a "sunset" law was passed which provided for the end (sunset) of all boards and commissions unless a convincing need for their continuation could be proved. This task, which was to be completed in six years, was more than budget or personnel could accomplish and the six years elapsed before the task was finished. More successful has been the attempt to include a sunset clause in all bills creating boards or commissions.

Although there are often problems with the operation and perhaps excessive number of boards and commissions, they serve to involve a large number of citizens in grassroots participation in government. Also, the importance of Arkansas boards and commissions cannot be underestimated in that the ordinary citizen may have more contact with a board or commission than with other governmental units.

All boards and commissions must operate in compliance with the provisions of the Freedom of Information Act and, unless specifically exempt, they must also conform to the provisions of the Administrative Procedure Act. The Administrative Procedure Act directs agencies to adopt organizational and operational rules, which are reviewed by the Legislative Council and the attorney general. All actions of boards and commissions are published in *The Arkansas Register,* a monthly publication of the secretary of state, and some boards and commissions must make certain proposed rules and regulations and other documents available at libraries throughout the state that have been designated "public depositories." These steps are taken to give the public a better understanding of board and commission operations and keep the various executive branch actors responsible to the citizenry.

Comparison to Other States

As noted earlier, a distinctive feature of the Arkansas state bureaucracy is the lack of merit system protections for state employees. As a right-to-work state, Arkansas does not provide the same degree of job security as do the federal government and many other states.

Another important feature of the Arkansas bureaucracy is numerous boards and commissions. These boards and commissions are staffed by a large number of state citizens. This service gives Arkansans an opportunity to gain insight about governmental operations.

Overall, Arkansas' state bureaucratic structure is like that of other states. Some state executive branches may be more streamlined with fewer independent commissions and agencies; however, the major functions and tasks are very similar. In addition, the quality of state employees remains a concern for most attentive citizens. As long as state and local personnel provide most of the face-to-face governmental service delivery, they remain important political actors, worthy of study and evaluation.

Additional Resources

Arkansas Government Agencies
http://www.arkansas.gov/government_name.php

The Council of State Governments
http://www.csg.org

The Judicial Branch

Chapter 5

In her leading work, *Arkansas Government and Politics*, Diane Blair noted that reformers sought three major revisions in the state court system. One was the consolidation and simplification in the court's structure. A second goal was centralized management and budgeting for the judicial branch. A third goal was minimal judicial education and qualifications for court personnel. (Blair, 1997: 192-94) With the passage of Amendment 80 and the continuing activities of the Administrative Office of the Courts, significant steps have been taken to achieve these goals. This is especially true concerning efforts to simplify the court's structure. Overall, no Arkansas government branch has undergone as many changes as the state judiciary.

Judiciary Concepts

Jurisdiction. State court systems usually have two types of jurisdiction – original and appellate. Original jurisdiction means a court has the power to be the first judicial body to hear a case. No verdict has been recorded in the case before it reaches the court. Appellate jurisdiction means a case has been heard before, and an official ruling has been rendered in the proceeding. It is this ruling that is reviewed by the court. In addition, appellate jurisdiction is usually discretionary. In other words, dissatisfied litigants may have the right to appeal, but the appeals court is free to accept or reject this request for review.

Courts. Most state court systems have two major types of courts – trial and appellate. Trial courts have original jurisdiction, while appellate courts usually exercise appellate jurisdiction.

In Arkansas and most states, there are two types of trial courts. These are trial courts of limited jurisdiction and trial courts of general jurisdiction. Trial courts of limited jurisdiction have original jurisdiction over specialized areas, like small claims and traffic offenses. Trial courts of general jurisdiction deal with the most important civil and criminal cases. It is in these courts where juries would be impaneled to hear evidence in a trial. Moreover, trial courts of general jurisdiction may also hear cases from trial

In This Chapter

Judiciary Concepts

Structure of the Arkansas Court System

Court Personnel

Administrative Office of the Courts

Comparison to Other States

Terms to Know

original jurisdiction

appellate jurisdiction

trial courts

appellate courts

intermediate appellate courts

supreme courts

civil cases

criminal cases

felonies

misdemeanors

courts of limited jurisdiction. This may occur if the state in question does not require limited jurisdiction courts to be courts of record. That is, no official record is kept of the proceedings in the trial court of limited jurisdiction.

In addition, Arkansas and most states have two types of appellate courts. These are intermediate appellate courts and supreme courts (courts of last resort). The intermediate appellate courts hear cases on appeal from lower trial courts. The focus of their legal review is whether the law was accurately applied to this situation. That is, did the lower court correctly interpret the legal precedent? The appellate court does not usually review the facts of the case. Although the bulk of state supreme courts' workloads is appellate proceedings, most state courts of last resort are provided some situations where they have original jurisdiction. These situations may involve intergovernmental disputes or circumstances where a timely response is needed to carry out a policy. For example, the Arkansas Supreme Court has original jurisdiction regarding proposed constitutional amendments. It also decides whether a constitutional amendment is appropriate and whether it should remain on the election ballot.

Cases. Legal proceedings are either civil cases or criminal cases. Civil cases usually involve controversies between individuals, between corporations, or between individuals and corporations in respect to private rights and obligations. The goal of many civil cases is economic compensation. Those bringing the controversy into court are called the plaintiffs and those being sued are called the defendants. Criminal cases involve the state or municipality against an individual alleging the individual has committed an offense against society by violating criminal laws. The criminal defendant receives many more legal protections than the civil defendant. Criminal cases fall into two categories – felonies and misdemeanors. Felonies are the more serious crimes punishable by large fines and/or imprisonment in the state penitentiary, or death. Misdemeanors are less serious offenses punishable by smaller fines and/or imprisonment in the county or city jails.

Judicial Selection. States utilize a variety of techniques to choose judicial personnel. Judges may be selected by partisan election (Democratic and Republican party labels); nonpartisan election; merit plan; gubernatorial appointment; or legislative selection. In addition, some states utilize one method for trial court selection while opting for a different approach for their appellate courts. (*The Book of the States*, 2008: 235, 247-50) Most Arkansas courts use the same selection method for state judges - nonpartisan election. The only exception is city court judges. Prior to the passage of Amendment 80, the state elected judges on a partisan basis. It should be noted that although judges are elected in nonpartisan contests, some judicial personnel are still picked in partisan competition. For example, prosecuting attorneys are chosen in this manner. Another interesting feature is that elected officials in the state judiciary are not term limited. Arkansas judges can hold office as long they maintain public support.

Juries. There are two kinds of juries in Arkansas – grand and petit. Grand juries do not hear individual cases, but are called to determine whether enough evidence exists to warrant cases going to trial. Petit juries are used in trials to determine the facts of a case. Any registered voter or owner of a drivers' license who is a resident of the county in which he or she may be summoned for jury service is legally qualified to act as a grand or petit juror if not otherwise disqualified. Beginning January 1, 2005, Act 1404 of 2003 expands the jury pool to include licensed drivers who have the usual juror qualifications: (1) U.S. citizen, (2) at least 18 years of age, (3) resident of the applicable county, and (4) no felony offenses.

Jury selection begins during the month of November or December of each year. At this time the circuit judge, in the presence of the circuit clerk, selects random numbers between one and 100. This list is sent to the county clerk's office. Then, the individual on the voter registration list with that number and every 100th person thereafter is placed on the Jury Master List until the minimum number required by law, or more, is reached. For example, if 33 is selected, the names of the 33rd, the 133rd, the 233rd, the 333rd, etc. persons on the voter registration list will be placed on the master list. (A.C.A. 16-32-103)

After all the names have been selected for the master list, the circuit judge, along with circuit clerk, pulls numbers from a large jury wheel. These numbers will be sent to the county clerk to cross-reference with the master list. The names and addresses from these numbers are sent back to the circuit clerk. The circuit clerk sends jury questionnaires to these individuals. The selected citizens answer the questionnaire and return it to the circuit judge's office. The circuit judge then reads the questionnaires and decides who should and should not serve on the jury list based on qualifications described in the questionnaires. This list is called the Petit Jury List.

Notification of a person selected to serve on a jury may be by: (1) a notice from the sheriff sent by first class mail; (2) notification personally by telephone; or (3) "any other method permitted or prescribed by law." (A.C.A. 16-32-106) A prospective juror who does not respond to a summons may be fined for this failure. At the discretion of the trial judge, people may be excused from jury duty. Some individuals are disqualified from serving by law. Those excluded are mentally retarded or insane persons; those unable to read or write (although these requirements may be waived by the judge); persons unable to speak or understand the English language, persons whose senses of hearing or seeing are substantially impaired; or "persons who are not of good character or approved integrity, are lacking in sound judgment or reasonable information, are intemperate, or not of good behavior."

(A.C.A. 16-31-106) People may be excused from jury duty or granted a deferment of service at the discretion of the trial judge. Except by consent of both parties, no person shall serve as a petit juror who is related to one of the attorneys in the case, is expected to appear as a witness, has already formed an opinion on the case, has material interest in the outcome of the case, is biased or prejudiced toward any of the participants, or has served as a petit juror in a former trial involving the same questions of fact.

The petit jury is used in civil and criminal cases. Jury trials are only conducted in the circuit courts. A different petit jury is chosen for each case from persons appearing in court that day. The circuit judge draws enough numbers from a jury wheel or box. The number of names drawn is influenced by whether the case is such that many prospective jurors might be disqualified or excused from serving. Most trials require juries of 12 persons. However, the legislature in 1993 permitted cases other than felonies to be tried, at the discretion of the trial court judge, by a jury of six jurors. (A.C.A. 16-19-604) In cases with 12 jurors, 12 names are drawn for each case. The prosecution and the defense attorneys question these potential jurors and may remove a set number of jurors during this phase. This process is referred to as striking a juror. Each party may make strikes. Then the number of strikes made is the number of new members called. Then the strike process starts over, until 12 jurors are seated or a party runs out of strikes. For six-person juries, names of 12 persons are drawn, each party strikes three names, and the remaining six serve. Petit jurors hear the evidence and, in civil cases, render verdicts for the plaintiff or the defendant; and in criminal cases, render verdicts of guilty or not guilty. In criminal cases the decision must be unanimous. The judge imposes the sentence although the jury may recommend a sentence. In civil cases, the jury awards damages. Only nine jurors need agree for a verdict to be reached in civil cases. (Amendment 16)

The grand jury serves several functions, but it usually deals with criminal matters. Grand jurors study the evidence in cases to determine if there is enough evidence to warrant prosecutions. If so, they make formal accusations of wrongdoing called indictments or true bills. A grand jury may also be called to investigate some undesirable situation in the area, such as a drug traffic problem, a question of election irregularities, possible illegal activity by an elected official, or the conduct of county business. It may also be asked to inspect public accounts or records. The circuit judge calls grand juries, but the judge may be responding to a request from other political actors. That is, the prosecuting attorney may request that a grand jury be called to investigate potential wrongdoing by a public official. For example, in 2003, a tentative request was made to call a grand jury to investigate election problems in Pulaski County.

Those serving on either a petit or grand jury may not be compelled to serve for more than 24 days or for more than a six month period in one year except when a trial is in progress at the termination of that period. After being excused at the conclusion of their service, they are ineligible to serve again in the same county for a period of two years. Any person summoned to jury duty may not be discharged from employment, may not lose sick leave or vacation time, or be penalized otherwise for their absence from work.

Structure of the Arkansas Court System

The Arkansas courts experienced significant structural changes due to the passage of Amendment 80. The new system reduced the number of trial courts of limited jurisdiction from six to two. In addition, the proposal eliminated separate courts of law and court of equity, a practice that now remains in only three states. Moreover, structural consolidation cut the number of trial courts of general jurisdiction from two to one. At the appellate level, Arkansas maintains a single court of appeals and one supreme court. These changes enabled more unified court procedures and clarified appropriate courts.

Trial Courts of Limited Jurisdiction. Arkansas has two types of trial courts of limited jurisdiction – district courts and city courts.

Each county has at least one district court, and if there is only one court in the county, it has county-wide jurisdiction. It should be noted that district judges may serve in more than one county. Qualifications for those who serve on the district courts include professional and residency requirements. All district judges must be licensed attorneys in Arkansas for at least fours years before taking office. In addition, they must reside in the geographic area they represent. District judges are elected to four-year terms. These courts have jurisdiction over misdemeanor cases, preliminary felony cases and civil cases in matters of less that $5,000. In addition, the district courts have a small claims division. This small claims provision provides citizens an opportunity to settle minor civil claims without the need and expense of legal representation. The district courts are designed to be the primary trial courts of limited jurisdiction.

City courts are a holdover from Arkansas' previous court structure. They tend to exist in smaller Arkansas communities. The mayor or the mayor's designee serves as judge in city courts. The mayor's designee must be a licensed attorney and reside in the county where the city is located. Unlike all other Arkansas courts, the city court judges are not explicitly required to have legal training. However, all city mayors have selected a designee to serve as judge rather than playing this role themselves. Therefore, from a practical standpoint, all judges do have legal qualifications. Another unique feature of city courts is the selection process. While judges in nonpartisan elections staff all other state courts, city court judges are appointed positions. The jurisdiction of city courts extends only to those situations that occur within the city. That is, city courts have exclusive jurisdiction of all prosecutions and actions for infractions of city bylaws or city ordinances. In addition, they have concurrent jurisdiction with the circuit courts and district courts of prosecutions for misdemeanors committed in the town or city.

Trial Courts of General Jurisdiction. Circuit courts are the most important trial courts in the Arkansas legal system. They handle the majority of original jurisdiction cases and most state legal disputes are resolved at this court level. Moreover, jury proceedings are conducted in the circuit courts. Each judge is elected circuit-wide in a nonpartisan election. Qualifications for those who serve on the circuit courts include professional and residency requirements. All circuit judges must be licensed attorneys in Arkansas for at least six years before taking office. In addition, they must reside in the circuit area they represent. Circuit judges are elected to a six-year term. These courts have five subject matter divisions: criminal, civil, probate, domestic relations, and juvenile. They have jurisdiction over most criminal and civil disputes as well as cases involving estates, adoptions, guardianships, neglect, delinquency, and Families in Need of Services (FINS). As noted earlier, these courts are where the bulk of legal work is done in the Arkansas court system.

Intermediate Appellate Court. The Arkansas Court of Appeals was created in 1978 to address the increasing workload of the Arkansas Supreme Court. There was a growing concern that the state supreme court would soon be unable to deal with the expanding number of cases on its docket. An intermediate appellate court was seen as a way to address this problem. Early evaluation indicates the action was successful because this court has stabilized the supreme court's workload. (*Arkansas Judiciary Annual Report*, 2001) Initially the court of appeals had six judges, but in 1993 the General Assembly passed legislation to add six additional judges. Three judges were added in 1995 and an additional three in 1996. Since the size of the court was doubled in a short period of time, some administrative and electoral issues arose. One was that judges are to serve staggered terms so a degree of continuity is preserved on the court. Another issue was that judicial districts had not been redrawn since the 1970 census, and population shifts created inequities in the districts. In 2003, the legislature addressed these issues by creating seven judicial districts and altering the terms for certain positions to establish a dispersed electoral selection pattern. (Act 1812 of 2003)

Today there are seven judicial districts and twelve judges serving on the Arkansas Court of Appeals. Two judges are elected in five districts and the remaining districts each elect one judge. Judges are required to be residents of the district from which they are elected. Technically, court of appeals judges must meet the same criteria as those individuals serving on the state supreme court. All court of appeals judges must be licensed attorneys in Arkansas for at least eight years before taking office, and each serves an eight-year term. The chief justice of the state supreme court designates one of the court of appeals judges to serve as chief judge. The appointment as chief judge is for a four-year term, and the person so named is eligible for reappointment.

The Arkansas Court of Appeals jurisdiction is determined by the Arkansas Supreme Court. Currently, it has appellate jurisdiction over those lower court cases not within the appellate jurisdiction of the supreme court. In addition, judgments of the court of appeals may be appealed to the supreme court whenever a case was erroneously filed in the Court of Appeals; a case filed in the Court of Appeals is believed to be of special public interest and is "certified" to the supreme court; or a case was decided by a tie vote. The supreme court may choose to hear some cases decided by the court of appeals, but it is not bound to do so. In fact, the supreme court rarely reviews cases decided by the court of appeals. The supreme court may transfer cases from the court of appeals to the supreme court, or vice versa. The court is authorized to divide itself into divisions of three judges each for the purpose of hearing cases, but no judge is assigned to any one panel permanently. Judges are rotated at least semiannually. A decision made by the panel is final, unless one judge dissents. In that situation, the case is heard and decided by all judges. Salaries for judges of the court of appeals are set by the General Assembly and paid by the state.

State Court of Last Resort. The Arkansas Supreme Court was established by the Constitution of 1836, and continued by the state's later constitutions, as the court to which decisions of all courts of general jurisdiction would be appealed. This was altered somewhat by the creation of the Arkansas Court of Appeals in 1978. Most cases come to the state supreme court under its statewide appellate jurisdiction. Such cases include appeals from lower courts involving constitutional issues and acts, municipal and county ordinances, rules of courts, administrative agency cases, criminal convictions of death, life, or more than 30 years imprisonment, post conviction relief petitions, election cases, and the law of torts. In addition, the state supreme court has appellate jurisdiction over those appeals certified for review from the court of appeals. The state supreme court also exercises original jurisdiction in certain subject areas. For example, the court has original jurisdiction to determine the legal status of state initiative and referendum petitions. However, the court's appellate jurisdiction continues to be its primary litigation source.

The Arkansas Supreme Court is composed of a chief justice and six associate justices, all of whom are elected in statewide nonpartisan elections. They serve eight-year terms that are staggered to preserve some degree of stability in court personnel. To be qualified to run for the position of justice, a person must meet citizenship, age, professional, and residency requirements. All Arkansas Supreme Court judges must be U.S. citizens and be at least thirty years old. Moreover, they must be practicing attorneys in Arkansas for at least eight years before taking office and have resided at least two years in Arkansas. The chief justice plays an important part in Arkansas court administration. This individual is designated to be the head of the judicial branch and plays a significant role in the Administrative Office of the Courts. (Act 3 of 2003)

Arkansas Court Structure

Source: Arkansas Judiciary

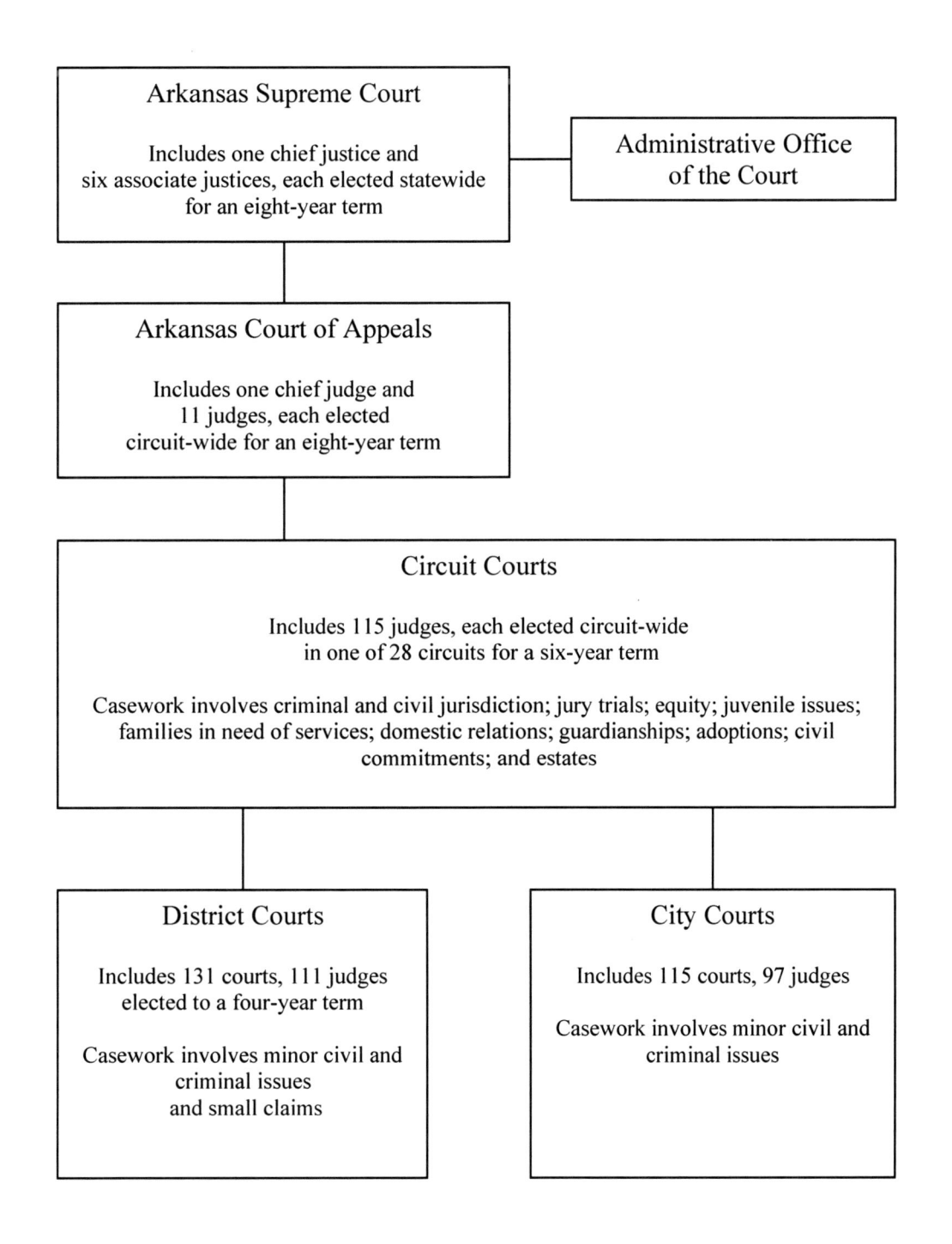

Arkansas Supreme Court

Includes one chief justice and
six associate justices, each elected statewide
for an eight-year term

Administrative Office of the Court

Arkansas Court of Appeals

Includes one chief judge and
11 judges, each elected
circuit-wide for an eight-year term

Circuit Courts

Includes 115 judges, each elected circuit-wide
in one of 28 circuits for a six-year term

Casework involves criminal and civil jurisdiction; jury trials; equity; juvenile issues; families in need of services; domestic relations; guardianships; adoptions; civil commitments; and estates

District Courts

Includes 131 courts, 111 judges
elected to a four-year term

Casework involves minor civil and
criminal issues
and small claims

City Courts

Includes 115 courts, 97 judges

Casework involves minor civil and
criminal issues

Arkansas Circuit Court Districts

Source: Arkansas Judiciary

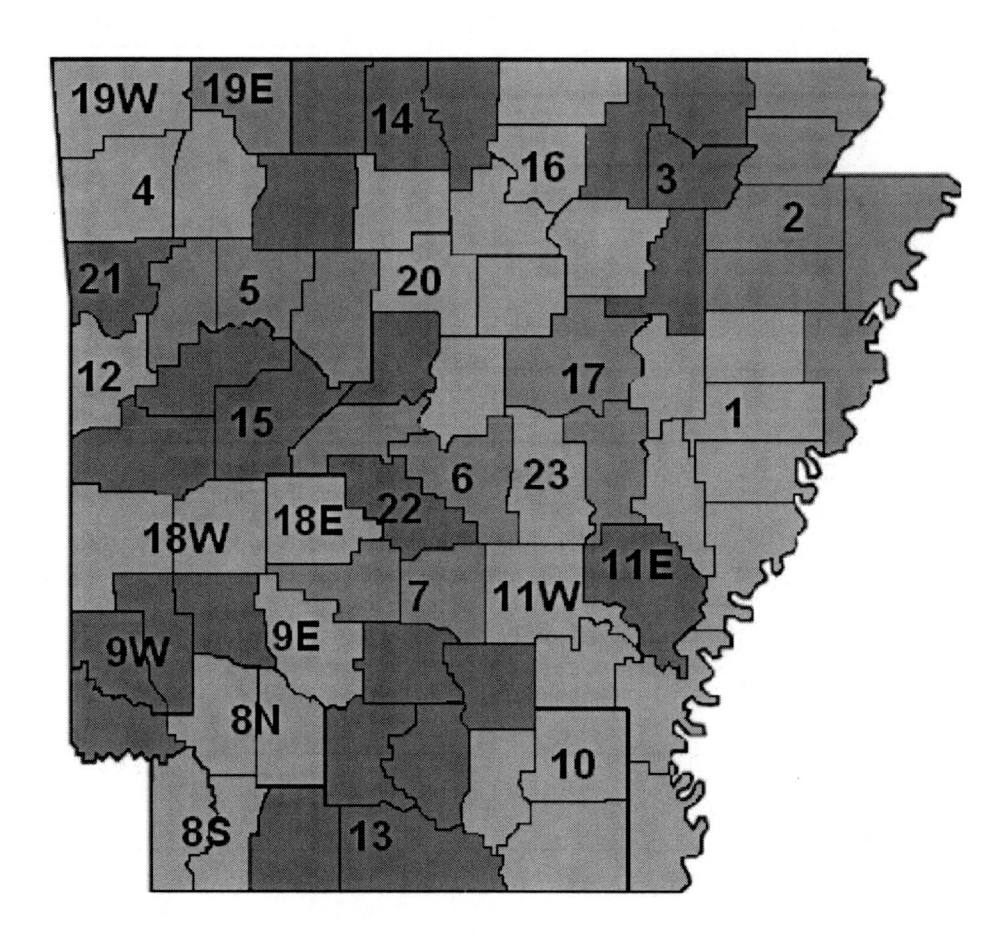

Arkansas Circuit Courts		
Circuit	Counties	Judges
1	Cross, Lee, Monroe, Phillips, St. Francis, Woodruff	5
2	Clay, Craighead, Crittenden, Greene, Mississippi, Poinsett	10
3	Jackson, Lawrence, Randolph, Sharp	3
4	Madison, Washington	6
5	Franklin, Johnson, Pope	4
6	Perry, Pulaski	17
7	Grant, Hot Spring	2
8N	Hempstead, Nevada	2
8S	Lafayette, Miller	3
9E	Clark	1
9W	Howard, Little River, Pike, Sevier	2
10	Ashley, Bradley, Chicot, Desha, Drew	5
11E	Arkansas	1
11W	Jefferson, Lincoln	6
12	Sebastian	6
13	Calhoun, Cleveland, Columbia, Dallas, Ouachita, Union	6
14	Baxter, Boone, Marion, Newton	4
15	Conway, Logan, Scott, Yell	3
16	Cleburne, Fulton, Independence, Izard, Stone	4
17	Prairie, White	3
18E	Garland	4
18W	Montgomery, Polk	1
19E	Carroll	1
19W	Benton	5
20	Faulkner, Searcy, Van Buren	4
21	Crawford	2
22	Saline	3
23	Lonoke	2
Source: Arkansas Judiciary		

Court Personnel

In addition to the judges of the various courts, attorneys and support personnel are essential to the operation of the courts.

Prosecuting Attorneys. Each judicial circuit has one prosecuting attorney who is elected by the people for a four-year term. Previously, prosecutors served a two-year term, but this was changed by recent constitutional reform. Another distinctive feature for prosecutors is the election method. While Amendment 80 altered the selection process for most judges to nonpartisan election, prosecutors are still chosen in partisan contests. Prosecuting attorneys must be United States citizens, have practiced law for at least four years before their election, and be residents of their respective circuit districts. It is the duty of the prosecuting attorney to commence and prosecute actions, both civil and criminal, in which the state or any county in the circuit may be involved. They also defend all suits brought against the state or county in their areas and give legal opinions and advice to all county officials. Unless a quorum court, by ordinance, establishes an office of county attorney, they also serve as legal counsel to the quorum court. They may appoint deputies to assist them.

Public Defenders. Following decisions by the United States Supreme Court requiring that a person accused with a serious offense must be provided counsel even if that person cannot afford an attorney, some counties in Arkansas employed public defenders, but most operated under a system established by the state of appointing and compensating attorneys for serving as counsel for indigent defendants. However, the U.S. Supreme Court struck down this system in 1992, and the General Assembly responded by establishing a trial public defender program throughout the state. The cornerstone of this system is the Public Defender Commission. This commission is composed of seven members appointed by the Governor for terms of five years. It hires an executive director and staff who are responsible for establishing policies and standards for the public defender system throughout the state. (A.C.A. 16-87-202 and 16-87-302)

The Public Defender Commission assigns public defenders throughout the state based upon county or district population, number of case filings, and other related factors. Each judicial district has at least one public defender, but many more may be assigned if it is warranted by caseloads. The trial public defenders are charged with defending indigent persons in all felony, misdemeanor, juvenile, guardianship, mental health cases, and traffic and contempt cases punishable by incarceration. In a case where there might be a conflict of interest or other reason why a trial public defender could not serve, the commission may reassign a different public defender or a private attorney to the case. However, state provisions are specific in stating that a private attorney should be used only as a last resort.

The trial public defender positions may be full or part-time jobs. If attorneys serve part-time, they may continue a general law practice. However, all full-time public defenders must give up their private practice. The commission is responsible for maintaining a list of attorneys who are qualified and willing to serve. It is also responsible for oversight of the Capital, Conflicts and Appellate Office. In order to pay for this system, the legislature added a fee in all civil and most criminal cases. Eighty percent of the funds collected by this fee may be used by the county; twenty percent is sent to the state treasurer to be deposited in the Public Defender Fund. Counties are also given permission to levy an additional fee to cover the cost. (A.C.A 14-20-102, 16-87-301, 16-87-302, and 16-87-307)

Court Reporters. All courts of general jurisdiction employ court reporters to record all court proceedings and to prepare and transcribe court transcripts.

Court Secretaries. Most courts also have court secretaries, who perform such secretarial duties as may be necessary for operation of the courts.

Case Coordinators. All judicial districts use case coordinators to assist trial judges with their case flow management by performing such tasks as maintaining the court calendar and dockets, setting cases for trial, scheduling hearings, and preparing reports. In some courts, the position of case coordinator is combined with the position of court reporter.

Administrative Office of the Courts

The Arkansas Supreme Court is not only the highest appeals court in the state, but the constitution gives it "general superintending control over all inferior courts of law and equity" and declares that it "shall make rules regulating the practice of law and professional conduct of attorneys at law." (Amendment 28) However, because of the election of judges and the comparative autonomy of the various lower courts, "general superintending control" by the state Supreme Court involves primarily supervision of caseloads and scheduling of cases rather than supervision of judges or the operation of the courts. Coordinating the Supreme Court's administrative functions is the Administrative Office of the Courts (formerly called the Judicial Department). This office is supervised by a director who is nominated by the chief justice, subject to approval by the Arkansas Supreme Court and the Judicial Council. The Judicial Council meets twice a year and is an advisory group composed of the justices of the Arkansas Supreme Court, judges of the Arkansas Court of Appeals, judges of the state's circuit courts, retired judges, and the director of the Administrative Office of the Courts.

The director of the Administrative Office of the Courts is charged with assisting the chief justice in carrying out the administrative responsibilities of the Arkansas Supreme Court. The principal functions of the office include collection, analysis, and publication of judicial statistics; arranging for continuous judicial education for all levels of personnel in the state's court system; and assisting the state supreme court boards and committees in the execution of their responsibilities. These boards and committees include the State Board of Law Examiners, which prepares the questions for the bar examination conducted twice yearly, grades the papers of those taking the examination, and certifies to the court the names of those who passed. The Continuing Legal Education Board assists in the ongoing judicial education effort for legal personnel. The Committee on Professional Conduct receives and investigates complaints against attorneys who are charged with professional misconduct. The Client Security Fund Committee is authorized to consider claims of clients who have suffered losses by reason of the dishonesty of attorneys who have represented them, and it may (within limits) pay such claims from a fund established by the Supreme Court. The Arkansas Court Appointed Special Advocates (CASA) promotes and supports local programs that provide qualified volunteer advocates to help abused and neglected children in juvenile dependency-neglect proceedings reach safe, permanent homes.

The Administrative Office of the Courts also responds to societal changes. One expanding role for this organization is the Court Interpreters Program. The office is responsible for matters related to foreign language interpreters for non-English speaking parties or witnesses in state and local courts of Arkansas. Another changing area is the use of technology under the auspices of the Committee on Automation. Currently, this committee is working on the Arkansas Court Automation Project (ACAP) with an ultimate goal of connecting all the Circuit Courts and District Courts to a statewide automated court system. Other committees involved with the practice of law in Arkansas are: the Committee on Civil Practice, Committee on Criminal Practice, Committee on Child Support, Committees on Model Jury Instructions – Civil and Criminal; the Board of Legal Specialization; and the Board of Certified Court Reporter Examiners. There is also a District Judges Council formed to promote the effectiveness of district courts, and a Code Revision Commission to provide continuing review, revision, codification and updating of the statutes.

Another important issue related to the judiciary is how to address situations where judges are suspected of misbehavior, become ill, or are unable to perform legal responsibilities. Until 1988, Arkansas had no effective method of disciplining judges or for handling disability of judges. In that year, the voters approved an amendment dealing with this problem. The General Assembly passed implementing legislation in 1989, which established the Arkansas Judicial Discipline and Disability Commission. This commission is composed of nine members: three are judges of Arkansas courts appointed by the state supreme court; three are Arkansas lawyers, one of whom is appointed by the attorney general, one by the president of the state senate, and one by the speaker of the state house; and three are neither judges nor lawyers and are appointed by the governor. (A.C.A. 16-10-402)

The Arkansas Judicial Discipline and Disability Commission's responsibilities include initiating and receiving information, conducting investigations and hearings, and making recommendations to the state supreme court regarding allegations of judicial misconduct, allegations of physical or mental disability of judges requiring leave or involuntary retirement, and matters of voluntary retirement or leave for disability. The legislation further provides for disciplinary measures ranging from granting of leave to suspension and removal from office. The state supreme court is responsible for adopting rules regarding the operation of the commission. The commission fills an important role in maintaining public confidence in the judicial branch.

Comparison to Other States

Structural reforms in Arkansas' court system were achieved with the passage of Amendment 80. Even though the new system replaced one of the most complex state court structures and provided a more unified and straightforward litigation process, not all members of the Arkansas Bar Association favored the re-organization.

Another important feature of any court system is the nature of judicial selection. The primary selection methods are partisan election, nonpartisan election, merit plan, gubernatorial appointment, and legislative selection. Comparing state supreme court selection methods, nine states use partisan elections; 14 states, including Arkansas, opt for nonpartisan elections; 16 states utilize a merit plan; seven states rely upon gubernatorial appointment; and four states employ legislative selection. (*Book of the States*, 2008: 247-250) In general, this means that 23 states use some form of competitive process, either partisan or nonpartisan elections. The remaining states rely upon some appointment or indirect process for judicial selection. Thus there is no dominant selection method for state supreme courts.

The shift away from partisan to nonpartisan elections is seen by many as a positive reform. However, even if candidates do not use party labels, there are still problems associated with a competitively elected judiciary. Candidates must still raise money to conduct their campaigns. This raises questions about campaign contributions and who might contribute. Also of concern are appropriate campaign issues for judicial races. For example, should judicial candidates discuss issues such as length of jail terms, sentencing guidelines, and treatment of prisoners? Finally, there is a concern that elections may not be the best selection method for evaluating the qualifications and temperament of judicial candidates. Amendment 80 provides explicit language that allows the legislature to submit merit plan selection for appellate judges to a vote of the people. Any merit plan would remove these judges from the competitive election process. This change may be a long time in coming, since there is no explicit timetable for such a proposal.

One important difference between Arkansas judicial candidates and individuals seeking a legislative or executive post is the lack of term limits for judicial office. While constitutional officers and state senators are limited to two four-year terms and state house members to three two-year terms, elected judicial personnel face no tenure restrictions. In addition, appellate court judges have longer terms (eight years) than any other elected official. A state supreme court justice who is elected to three terms should serve for 24 years; a state House member elected to the maximum three terms will serve only six years in office. Hence longer terms are the norm for judicial personnel.

Although there are still a number of possible reforms, these changes have reduced much of the overlapping jurisdictions and complexity in the state's legal system.

Additional Resources

Arkansas Judiciary
http://courts.state.ar.us

The Council of State Governments
http://www.csg.org

Local Government

In contrast to other public entities, local governments have the most direct impact on citizens' daily lives. Decision makers in municipalities and counties strongly influence people's most basic services, including water utilities, waste disposal, polling places, and tax collection. In addition, citizens are more likely to come in contact with a representative of local government. For these reasons, local governments remain a very important part of the state's political landscape.

County Government

County governments have long been one of the most important political entities for Arkansans. In fact, the 1874 Constitution has far more sections dealing with county than with municipal government. This is a reflection of Arkansas' rural character. Historically, counties were the most important governing element in agrarian states. Therefore, in the late nineteenth century, counties received a great deal of attention from political decision-makers.

Since 1874, there have been significant changes in structure and authority of counties. One of the major changes occurred with the passage of Amendment 55 in November 1974. This amendment, which became operationally effective in all 75 counties on January 1, 1977, granted home rule to the counties. By so doing, it made county government in Arkansas a creation of the constitution rather than of the legislature. The basic goal of home rule is to provide local decision makers the legal authority to make decisions without specific state legislative approval. The amendment states: "A county acting through its quorum court may exercise legislative authority not denied by the constitution or by law." Although the legislature may still deny counties certain powers, the legislature has no authority over those powers specifically granted counties by Amendment 55. However, since passage of Amendment 55, court decisions and enactment by the General Assembly of numerous laws

---

Chapter

6

In This Chapter

County Government

Municipal Government

Other Local Government Entities

Comparison to Other States

Terms to Know

annexation
circuit clerk
coroner
county assessor
county boards
county clerk
county collector
county judge
county surveyor
county treasurer
sheriff
home rule
incorporation
township

restricting the powers of the counties have made the concept of home rule less clear.

To implement Amendment 55, the General Assembly in 1977 passed the Arkansas County Government Code (Act 742), a 95-page document which "provides a comprehensive revision of the laws of the State relating to county government." It specifically addressed the legislative powers and procedures of the quorum court and the executive jurisdiction and powers of the elected county officials.

Quorum Court. A quorum court is the legislative assembly on the county level. Before 1977, quorum courts had been large and unwieldy with one justice of the peace for every 200 people. With the passage of Amendment 55, quorum courts in Arkansas are now composed of no fewer than nine and not more than 15 members, depending on the population size of the county. Following each federal decennial census (every 10 years), the county board of election commissioners divides the county into the appropriate number of single member districts so that each justice of the peace will represent "as nearly as practicable an equal number" of inhabitants. Practically, the U.S. Supreme Court has ruled that individuals' votes must have equal influence in choosing their officials. That is why lines must be redrawn or reapportioned to have the same number of citizens in each district. This reapportionment must be completed on or before January 1 of the second year after the census (2002, 2012, etc.).

The county judge, the county's chief executive, presides over the quorum court. Justices of the peace (JPs) are members of the quorum court. JPs must be qualified electors and residents of the districts from which they are elected. Unlike most Arkansas public officials, JPs are not required to meet additional age or residency requirements. For example, a county judge must be least 25 years old, but a quorum court member must be a qualified elector. This means a JP could be as young as 18 years old. The qualified voters of their districts elect JPs, and they serve two-year terms. Quorum court vacancies are filled by appointment by the governor.

The quorum court has general legislative authority allowing it to "adopt ordinances necessary for the government of the county." It is given specific powers such as setting the number and compensation of deputies and county employees, filling vacancies in elective county offices, appropriating public funds for county expenses, and levying taxes in a manner prescribed by law. The quorum court must provide certain necessary services for its citizens including the administration of justice through the courts, law enforcement protection, real and personal property tax administration, the keeping of court and public records, and management of the county's solid waste. Other services which the quorum court may provide include agricultural services, community and rural development services, county planning, parks, libraries, museums, civic centers, public camping grounds, emergency services, fire protection, juvenile services, pollution control, public health, recycling services, transportation, water, sewer and other utility services. The quorum court is specifically prohibited from enacting any legislation that is contrary to the general laws of the state, which is in conflict with the powers of municipalities, or which is the prerogative of the Arkansas General Assembly. It is also forbidden to declare any act a felony or to attach a fine of over $500 to any misdemeanor. These provisions may limit the efforts to give counties the decision-making discretion associated with home rule.

The quorum court must meet at least once a month. Either the county judge or a majority of the justices of the peace may call special meetings when necessary. *Per diem* compensation is paid to justices of the peace for attending any official, regular, special or committee meeting of the quorum court. The *per diem* rate is determined by the quorum court, but within limits established by state law.

Initiative and Referendum. The legislative powers granted the quorum court by Amendment 55 do not eliminate the power of the people, granted by Amendment 7 of the constitution, to enact legislation by initiative or to reject action taken by the quorum court through referendum. The process of petitioning for an initiative or referendum vote by the people is the same for counties as for the state, but such considerations as percentages, deadlines, and verification of signatures are different. (See Chapter 2.) Also, by a three-fifths vote of its total membership, a quorum court may refer any ordinance to a vote of the people for approval or rejection.

County Officers. The quorum court, through its authority to fix the number and compensation of deputies and county employees and its responsibility for appropriating all county funds, has considerable power to organize the general operation of county government. Amendment 55 also gave the quorum court the power to reorganize the various county departments if the people of the county vote to approve such action. However, Act 742 specifically excluded the office of county judge from being reorganized and placed some other restrictions on the reorganization process. Since 1977, a few counties have successfully combined departments, but attempts by other counties at major reorganization have been struck down by the Arkansas Supreme Court, which has maintained that any reorganization plan that does not provide adequate checks and balances is unconstitutional.

The Constitution of 1874 authorizes nine county officers, although all counties do not have all nine. All serve two-year terms. Their salaries are set by the quorum court, but must be within limits set by the General Assembly. Except for the county judge, the only qualifications for these offices are that candidates must be residents of the county and qualified electors. The county judge also must be at least 25 years of age, a citizen of the United States, "a person of upright character, of good business education, and a resident of the county at the time of his election and during his continuance in office." (A.C.A. 14-14-1301)

Primary administrative responsibility for the county rests with the county judge, who presides over the quorum court without a vote, but with the power of the veto. A vote of three-fifths of the total membership of the quorum court is required to override a veto. The county judge is responsible for county roads and is custodian of county property. The Constitution of 1874 also designated the county judge as judge of the county court, which was given "exclusive original jurisdiction in all matters relating to county taxes, roads, bridges, ferries, paupers, bastardy, vagrants, the apprenticeship of minors, the disbursement of money for county purposes, and in every other case that may be necessary to the internal improvement and local concerns of the respective counties." (VII, Sec. 28) Amendment 55 redefined some of these responsibilities, and Amendment 80 provided that all matters relating to juveniles and bastardy be assigned to circuit courts. However, the county judge still has some judicial responsibilities such as ruling on annexations.

The county clerk is the official bookkeeper of county records; the clerk is also the *ex officio* clerk of the county court; clerk of the board of equalization; and clerk of the quorum court in 73 counties (two counties have full-time quorum coordinators). In addition, the clerk may house the probate records, but this assignment rests with the local circuit judge. The county clerk serves as the permanent voter registrar and is in charge of absentee and early voting. Moreover, the county clerk also is responsible for issuing marriage licenses and recording county court proceedings, articles of incorporation, and new businesses. Finally, the clerk may prepare monthly delinquent tax lists. This is most common if the County Sheriff also performs the County Collector function.

The circuit clerk keeps the records of the circuit courts including those of the criminal, civil, domestic relations, and juvenile divisions. Another judicial role for the circuit clerk is jury selection. The clerk is also responsible for the filing of deeds, mortgages, powers of attorney, land records (plats and surveys), and uniform commercial code (UCC) records linked to farming. Today, all other UCC records are filed with the Secretary of State's office.

The sheriff is the principal peace officer of the county, making arrests for violation of laws; serving notices, subpoenas, and warrants; and serving as bailiff of the circuit and district courts. The sheriff is in charge of the county jail. In some counties, the sheriff also serves as tax collector.

The county collector gathers municipal, county, school, and improvement district taxes and turns them over to the county treasurer. The collector also prepares delinquent tax lists and collects delinquent taxes.

The county treasurer is responsible for the custody and disbursement of all funds collected by the county, including special funds, school district, and improvement district funds. The treasurer is responsible for remitting a portion of the county taxes to the cities and towns, and is a member of the County Depository Board, which invests funds not immediately needed. The treasurer must submit to the quorum court a monthly statement of the financial condition of the county.

The county assessor appraises real estate and personal property, and keeps appropriate records of same.

The coroner signs death certificates if there is no doctor present, and may hold inquests to establish the cause of deaths that may appear to have occurred by other than natural causes. In most counties, the office of coroner is not a full-time position.

The county surveyor locates property boundaries at the request of the assessor and settles boundary disputes if they are taken to court. This office also is not a full-time position.

Township Officers. Originally, counties were divided into townships of two types – geographical and political. Today, geographical townships are used only in surveying to locate and describe land boundaries. On the other hand, the original political townships are often used as election precincts and as boundaries for political district lines such as quorum court districts and state legislative districts. Two township officers are authorized by the constitution - justices of the peace (JPs) and constables. Originally, JPs were authorized to preside over justice of the peace courts and to perform other judicial duties prescribed by law. Today, although JPs are still officially township officers, none of them presides over justice of the peace courts, though some do exercise such judicial duties as performing marriages. The second township officer authorized is the constable. For election of constables, township lines are the same as quorum court district lines. The only qualifications for those running for the office are that they live in the township (quorum court district) they serve and are registered to vote.

County Revenues. Although it varies from county to county, over half of revenue received by most Arkansas counties today is from local sources. Federal funds come from grants-in-aid programs and payments in lieu of taxes (PILT) on federally owned lands in 51 counties. State funds are in the form of general turnback funds – taxes collected by the state and then turned back to local governments. These include: highway revenue turnback, state aid for secondary roads, sale of tax-forfeited land, revenue from forests and from sale of leases of lands in the public domain, and severance tax turnback. The primary county sources of revenue are the *ad valorem* tax on real and personal property; fees, fines, penalties, licenses, and charges for services rendered; the sales tax; and sale of bonds. Counties may also levy an income tax, but at present no county does.

County Expenditures. Before the beginning of each calendar year, the quorum court must adopt a budget indicating expected revenues and proposed expenditures for the following year. Expenditures may not be budgeted for more than 90% of estimated revenue. No county funds may be expended without specific appropriation of the quorum court. In general, counties spend between 25% and 30% of their revenue on roads and rural services; between 25% and 30% on law enforcement, including operation of a county jail; between 10% and 15% on courts and judicial administration; and the rest on administration, county buildings and general services, health and social services, elections, and emergency services.

County Boards. In addition to the quorum court and the county officials, there are administrative and advisory boards and commissions which participate in the operation of county government.

With certain exceptions, all administrative boards have five members who are appointed by the county judge and approved by the quorum court. Their terms are staggered with each member serving a five-year term. Administrative boards are created by quorum court ordinances and have such administrative and regulatory powers as granted them by county ordinance and permitted by state law. The number and type of administrative boards is optional with each county. However, if a county operates a hospital, it must have a Hospital Board of Governors. Other administrative boards include: Library Board, County Planning Board, Law Library Board, Rural Development Authority, County Depository Board, and County Board of Education.

Advisory boards may be of any size. Members are appointed by the county judge and often need not be approved by the quorum court. Advisory boards may or may not be created by county ordinance. Members have no specified term of office, unless determined by ordinance. Their duties and responsibilities are strictly advisory.

One county board mandated by state law is the County Equalization Board. This board meets regularly in August (and into September if necessary) to hear complaints from taxpayers who feel that their property has been unfairly assessed. A taxpayer dissatisfied with a decision made by the board may appeal to the county court. Board members serve three-year terms and are usually paid for their services. They must be qualified electors who "have been real property owners for at least one year." (A.C.A. 26-27-305) County Equalization Boards have three, five or nine members. This is based upon the number of judicial districts in the county and county population. If a County Equalization Board has three members, one member is chosen by the county judge, one by representatives of the cities and towns, and one by representatives of the school districts. If the Board has five members, three are appointed as above and two by majority vote of the quorum court. Finally, if the board has nine members, two members are chosen by the county judge, two by representatives of the cities and towns, two by representatives of the school districts, and three are chosen by a majority vote of the quorum court. The quorum court is expected to fill one of the three positions with a licensed real estate appraiser. If no appraiser is willing to serve, the court may choose a real estate broker, or failing in this effort, it may choose a real estate salesperson. (A.C.A. 26-27-302 and 26-27-304)

Intergovernmental Cooperation Councils. The legislature established these councils in 1987 to "encourage cooperation by the various local government jurisdictions within each county." Membership of each council consists of the county judge, who chairs the council and has both a vote and veto power; the county clerk, who serves as secretary; and the mayor of each city and incorporated town within the county. The legislature lists 13 different public services that must be reviewed by the council at least once during each year. The council is required to meet at least quarterly and to make an annual report to the Joint Interim Committee on City, County, and Local Affairs of the General Assembly. (A.C.A. 14-27-102 and 14-27-104)

Municipal Government

Understandably, when the writers of the constitution addressed local government, they included comparatively few sections relating to municipal government. In general, municipal governments in Arkansas do not have home rule. They are, instead, creations of the state with only those powers granted them by the constitution and by laws passed by the General Assembly. This legislative power of the General Assembly regarding cities and incorporated towns is stated in Article XII of the constitution: "The General Assembly shall provide, by general laws, for the organization of cities (which may be classified) and incorporated towns, and restrict their power of taxation, assessment, borrowing money and contracting debts, so as to prevent the abuse of such power." (XII, 3) In recent years, the concept of control by the legislature over the powers of municipalities has included passage by the General Assembly of legislation prohibiting municipalities from passing ordinances involving such issues as rent control, pesticides, and gun control.

Today, there are over 400 active incorporated cities and towns in Arkansas. These municipalities are legally corporations. They are distinguished from business corporations by being called public or municipal corporations, but any corporation is treated legally as a "person" with certain obligations, rights and privileges. A municipal corporation has such corporate rights as the capability of suing and being sued, of making contracts, and of acquiring, holding, and possessing property. Municipalities may also levy those taxes authorized by law, exercise all powers conferred by the constitution and the legislature, and provide municipal services.

Originally municipal services consisted of little more than fire and police protection, but today these services may include sanitation, water, sewers, utilities, streets, libraries, hospitals, museums, parks and recreation programs, social services, emergency medical services, and many others. In Arkansas, school districts are separate from municipal governments although there is frequently cooperation between the two. The geographic boundaries of school districts seldom coincide with the boundaries of municipalities.

Incorporation. For a city or town to be incorporated, a written petition must be prepared which describes the geographic area involved and identifies the person or persons authorized to act on behalf of the petitioners. The petition must be signed by not less than 75 qualified electors and presented to the county court (county judge). If approved by the county court, a hearing is held to air any objections to the incorporation of such a town or city. If there are no objections, the incorporation is filed with the secretary of state, and notice of election of officers for the newly incorporated municipality is posted. New cities or towns cannot incorporate if they are within five miles of the boundaries of another incorporated city or town unless that city's governing body has "by written resolution affirmatively consented to said incorporation" or a natural barrier exists making the area to be incorporated inaccessible to the existing municipality. (A.C.A. 14-38-101)

Annexation. Whenever a majority of the real estate owners of an area adjoining a town or city (provided such majority own at least one-half of the acreage affected) wish to be annexed to that town or city, they may file a petition with the county court. A hearing must be held by the county court within 30 days of the filing of the petition. Following the hearing, another 30 days must be allowed for objections to annexation. If there are no objections, annexation is recorded, and unless the town or city refuses to accept the territory, the territory becomes, by ordinance of the city council, a part of the town or city.

When a municipality wishes to annex land contiguous to it, the governing body of that municipality may, by a two-thirds vote of the city council or board of directors, adopt an ordinance to annex those lands. The annexation ordinance must be submitted to a vote of the qualified voters in the annexing municipality and in the area to be annexed. This ordinance must contain an accurate description of the land to be annexed and a schedule of services that will be extended to the area within three years after the date of annexation. To pass, it must be approved by a majority of the total votes cast. The votes in the city and those in the proposed annexation area are not counted separately. Should two cities wish to annex the same territory, both cities must hold elections and, if annexation is approved for both cities, a third election shall be called. Only those living in the territory to be annexed may vote, and their decision is final. (A.C.A. 14-30-302 and 14-30-303)

Classification. Incorporated municipalities in Arkansas are classified according to population size. First class cities are those having 2,500 or more inhabitants; second class cities have at least 500 inhabitants, but less than 2,500; those with under 500 are incorporated towns. Powers granted to municipalities vary with their classification. Once a municipality reaches the population of 500, it must be classified a second class city, and once a municipality reaches 2,500, it must be classified a first class city. However, if the citizens of a town of under 500 inhabitants wish to become a second class city, they may do so by adoption and publication of an appropriate ordinance. Also any city of 1,500 or more may, by enactment of an ordinance, become a first class city. (A.C.A. 14-37-103)

Forms of Government. There are three forms of municipal government used in Arkansas: mayor-council (also called aldermanic), city manager, and city administrator. All towns and second-class cities have mayor-council governments. All first-class cities have the mayor-council form of government unless a petition signed by 15% of the number of voters who cast votes for mayor in the preceding election is filed with the mayor, asking that the people vote on the proposition that a different form of government be adopted. If such a proposition passes, the city is reorganized and the question of changing the form of government cannot be resubmitted to the people for another six years. If the proposition fails, the question may not be resubmitted to the people for another four years.

A majority of Arkansas cities and towns use the mayor-council system, whereas five cities use the city manager form and three have a city administrator.

Mayor-Council Form. The corporate authority of a town or city using the mayor-council form of government rests with an elected mayor, an elected council, and such other elected or appointed officials as authorized by law. There are no special qualifications for those running for city office except that they must be residents of the city or town and, in case of aldermen, they must be residents of the ward which they represent. City attorneys and district judges must be licensed to practice law. Candidates may run as nominees of political parties or may file as independents. The constitutional provision that prohibits persons appointed to office from running for that office does not apply to municipal offices. In mayor-council municipalities, all officials run at large, except aldermen who may be elected at large or, by ordinance of the city council, from wards by those residing in the wards. (Amendment 29)

The mayor of a city is its "chief executive officer and conservator of its peace." The mayor is *ex officio* president of the city council and presides at its meetings. The mayor has a vote "when needed to pass an ordinance, bylaw, resolution, order or motion" and has the power of the veto. The veto must take place within five days after passage of an ordinance by the city council. Before the next regular meeting of the council, the mayor must file in the office of the city clerk a written statement giving reasons for the veto. At the next meeting, the mayor's veto may be overridden by a two-thirds vote of the council.

The mayor appoints all of the municipality's department heads unless the city or town council members override the mayor's appointment by a two-thirds vote of its total membership. Most other appointments by the mayor require simple majority approval by the council. The mayor is also a member of certain administrative and quasi-judicial boards and commissions, including pension boards, sanitation and health boards, and others. In case of a vacancy in the office of mayor, second-class city councils may fill the vacancy by appointing a replacement or by calling a special election. In first class cities, the city council is required to call a special election if the unexpired term has more than six months to run. The vacancy may be filled by vote of the council if less than six months remains in the term. In case of a vacancy in the office of alderman, the city council elects a replacement unless it is in a city with a population of over 50,000. In that case, if the unexpired term exceeds one year, a special election shall be called. Vacancies in all other offices are filled by vote of the city councils. In incorporated towns, the town council fills all vacancies.

The city or town council is responsible for management and control of the municipality's finances and of all real and personal property belonging to the town. It has legislative authority to enact ordinances "...necessary for the good government of the city and for the due exercise of its corporate power..." (A.C.A. 14-43-502)

Salaries of the mayor, aldermen, and other officials are fixed by the governing body or the municipality, in accordance with Amendment 56 of the Arkansas Constitution, which states that salaries shall not exceed limits established by law. They may be increased, but not decreased during the term for which the officials have been elected or appointed.

City Manager Form. Only first-class cities with a population of at least 2,500 may adopt the city manager form of government. All executive and legislative authority in this form of government rests with an elected board of directors, including a mayor elected by the other directors, or with an elected board of directors and an elected mayor. There are four optional methods for electing directors:
- all members of the board may be elected at large;
- an odd number of directors, including the mayor, with any combination of directors, may be elected at large or from wards;
- all members elected from wards except mayor, who is elected at large;
- all members elected from wards.

The directors choose the mayor unless a method of election is approved by a majority vote of the city's electors. The electors may require directors to be elected by a majority vote or by an approved minimum vote of less than 50%. In the first case, if no candidate receives a majority of the votes, a runoff election involving the top two candidates is required. In the second case, the candidate receiving the approved minimum number of votes and the most votes is elected mayor. If no candidate receives the minimum percentage, a runoff election of the top two candidates is held.

An elected mayor may, by a vote of the qualified voters of the city, be given veto power but no vote unless there is a tie. A veto may be overridden by a two-thirds vote of the council. (A.C.A. 14-43-504 and 14-44-107)

To be qualified for election as a director or mayor, a person must have resided in the city for 30 days, be "more than 21 years of age," and be a qualified elector. If a city has chosen to elect directors from wards, the candidates must live in the wards they plan to represent. Each candidate must file a petition with the city clerk that has been signed by at least 50 qualified electors. It must be filed not more than 60 or less than 40 days before the election. All elections are non-partisan. All terms of office are for four years. If a vacancy should occur in the office of director or mayor, the board of directors, by majority vote, elects a person to serve the unexpired term.

In the city manager form of government, neither the mayor nor the directors receive any compensation unless authorized by the voters of the city. The board is required to meet within the first and third weeks of each calendar month and may call special meetings when necessary. A majority of the board constitutes a quorum and a quorum is necessary for the transaction of business.

The procedure of recall may be used to remove the mayor or any director from office. The recall is accomplished by first filing a petition with the city clerk. The petition must be signed by a number of qualified electors equal to 35% of the total number of votes cast for that office in the preceding election. The city clerk must verify within ten days that the signatures are those of qualified electors and that there is a sufficient number of signatures. If the petition is determined to meet requirements, the city clerk notifies the board of directors, which then calls a special election to be held in not less than 30 days and not more than 40 days. A simple majority vote is necessary for removal. No recall petition may be filed against a director or mayor unless that person has served at least six months.

In the city manager form of government, the board of directors employs a city manager, who serves an indefinite term, and receives a salary determined by the board. Powers and duties of the city manager include supervision and control of administrative departments, agencies, offices, and employees; preparation of an annual budget and an annual financial report; advising the board of the financial condition and future needs of the city; and performing such additional duties and exercising such additional powers as may, by ordinance, be lawfully delegated to him by the board.

City Administrator Form. Any first-class city may adopt the city administrator form of government – seven elected directors and one elected mayor. The legislative and executive authority rests with the board of directors, subject to certain powers granted the mayor. The board is required to meet in regular sessions twice a month. The mayor presides over all board meetings and has the power of veto except in matters of personnel. The board may override the mayor's veto by an affirmative vote of five or more.

To be eligible to run for mayor or director, an individual must be at least 21 years of age, have resided within the municipality for at least six months, and be a qualified elector. A city with city administrator form of government is divided into four wards "composed of contiguous territory and of substantially equal population." The director positions are numbered 1, 2, 3, 4, 5, 6, and 7. The persons elected to fill positions 1, 2, 3, and 4 must be qualified electors of their respective wards and be elected by the qualified voters of those wards. Positions 5, 6, and 7 and the position of mayor are elected at large. All terms are for four years and all elections are non-partisan. Any person desiring to be a candidate must file a petition signed by at least 50 qualified electors of the city.

The mayor is not required to give full time to the office and may receive such salary or compensation as determined by the board of directors within limits set by law. Once the salary amount is set, however, it may not be increased or decreased during the term of office for which the mayor was elected. Directors receive compensation for their attendance at meetings, but not for special meetings. The board compensation "may not exceed 1/24 of 20% of the compensation permitted municipal offices." Any director failing to attend five consecutive regular meetings or 50% of the regular meetings held during a calendar year is deemed to have resigned. The procedure of recall, which may be used to remove the mayor or any director, is the same as that used in the city manager form of government.

In a city with administrator form of government, the board of directors employs a city administrator who serves at the pleasure of the board. The offices of treasurer, city clerk, city attorney, heads of departments, and city employees are filled by the administrator with the approval of the board of directors. It is also the city administrator's responsibility to supervise all city employees, departments, agencies, and offices, and to perform such other duties as may be assigned by the board of directors. Salaries of the city administrator and all city employees are determined by the board. (A.C.A. 14-48-109 and 14-48-110)

Initiative and Referendum. Amendment 7 grants citizens the right to enact state and county legislation through the initiative petition process and to reject acts by the General Assembly or the quorum court through the referendum petition process. This is also applicable to the municipal level of government. The procedure is the same as with state initiative and referendum petitions. (See Chapter 2 for the percentages, deadlines, and other specifications for municipal petitions.) Unlike state government, but like county government, municipal governments may decide to refer any ordinance to a vote of the people for their acceptance or rejection. The decision to do so, however, requires a two-thirds vote of a city council or board of directors as compared to only a three-fifths vote required of the quorum court.

Municipal Revenues. The primary monetary sources for municipal governments are local revenues. Most of the monies come from the local option sales tax, franchise taxes, fees, and the *ad valorem* property tax. The state of Arkansas is usually the second largest contributor to municipal government budgets. Primarily, the state provides funds from general municipal turnback and street turnback. The federal government also plays a role usually through grants-in-aid or loans. In general, federal contributions as a percent of Arkansas communities' budgets have declined over the last two decades. This has forced the municipalities to rely more upon local revenues. (See Chapter 10.)

Municipal Expenditures. The type of expenditures made by cities and towns in Arkansas varies considerably depending on the size of the municipality and the services offered. In general, however, between 25 and 30% of a city or town's general operating budget is spent on police protection, between 15 and 20% on fire protection, between 20 and 30% on streets, and the remainder on administration, health, parks and recreation, sanitation, libraries, emergency medical and other services. Water and sewer operations often involve major expenditures, but, if operated under a water and/or sewer commission, they are financed by user fees and charges, and financial accounting for them is separate from general municipal operations.

Boards and Commissions. The number of boards and commissions in a municipality depends on the nature of services provided. If a city or town participates in planning and zoning, a planning commission is usually created. If a municipality has a library, there is a library board. If there are municipally supported parks and recreational programs, there is a parks and recreation board. In first-class cities using a civil service system, a five-person civil service commission is appointed to supervise the city's civil service for the police and fire departments. If a city levies a gross receipts tax on hotels and restaurants, it must create a city advertising and promotion commission to oversee expenditures of the tax revenue.

Other boards municipalities may create include airport commissions, housing authorities or urban renewal agencies, arts or museum boards, port authorities, public facilities boards, city beautification committees, etc.

Other Local Government Entities

Over the years, regional and intergovernmental organizations have been created for a variety of reasons. Some of the earliest were improvement districts created for projects such as levee management and drainage control. Later, cooperative arrangements between units of government were developed in response to grant opportunities provided by the federal government. In 1955, Act 26 was passed, enabling creation of joint planning commissions by various combinations of adjacent counties, cities and towns. Examples include Metroplan (Pulaski and Saline Counties); Northwest Arkansas Regional Planning Commission (Benton and Washington Counties); Southeast Arkansas Regional Planning Commission (Pine Bluff-Jefferson County); and the Southwest Regional Planning Commission. These still exist but their function today is primarily accomplished through contracts with the local governments in their district to provide services in the areas of mapping, census taking, annexations, and city planning and zoning. (A.C.A. 14-17-302)

In the 1960s, a second type of area-wide planning agency developed in Arkansas as a result of the passage by the United States Congress of the Public Works and Economic Act. In order to receive funds under this act, eight Economic Development Districts (EDDs) were formed in Arkansas. Each district was required to include at least two redevelopment counties and at least one growth center city capable of fostering the economic growth activities necessary to alleviate adverse economic conditions in the district. Act 118 of 1969 expanded functions of EDDs from economic development only to include planning and renamed them Planning and Development Districts (PDDs). (A.C.A. 14-166-201) Although direct federal grants available to the PDDs are not as numerous as in the 1960s and 1970s, the eight districts solicit funds and grants in order to provide services and planning for agencies involved with problems of aging, housing, job training, regional jails and juvenile detention facilities, transportation planning and operations, and economic development.

In 1967, the "Interlocal Cooperative Act" was passed to give local government broad authority to create intergovernmental organizations to address area needs and projects. (A.C.A. 25-20-101) Over the years, this general law has been supplemented by separate laws which govern various types of projects such as regional airports, housing authorities, tourist promotion agencies, port authorities, regional jails and/or juvenile detention facilities, water distribution districts, industrial development agreements, and others.

While local units of government are not required to deal with problems through cooperative arrangements, other problems are considered of such importance statewide that the entire state is divided into districts with each district being responsible for implementation in their area of a state program. An example of such a problem is solid waste management. In 1989, the General Assembly passed legislation creating eight Solid Waste Planning Districts, whose boundaries coincided with the PDD boundaries. Subsequent legislation in 1991 changed their name to Solid Waste Management Districts and permitted counties to combine to form other management districts provided that there was more than one county in a district (unless a county had a population of 50,000 or more) and that two or more of the counties be adjacent to one another. Each district has primary responsibility for providing a solid waste management system for its district. This includes solid waste pick-up, resource recovery, and solid waste disposal. The state legislature gave the districts management control over landfills including watershed protection. It allowed the districts to adopt stricter standards for landfills and waste disposal operations than the state, if districts had an approved comprehensive land use plan in operation. (A.C.A. 8-6-703 and 8-6-209)

Other statewide problems addressed by regional councils and boards include the seven Resource Conservation and Development Councils, which operate under the state's conservationist. Numerous study committees are addressing state transportation problems and commissions, some mandated by federal legislation and some directed by the state.

Another type of regional government may cross state lines and deal with river basins or with economic development for areas such as the Delta region. Other examples are the three interstate planning agencies: the Mississippi-Arkansas-Tennessee Council of Government (MAT-COG); Arkansas-Texas Council of Governments (Texarkana); and Arkhoma Regional Planning Commission (Fort Smith).

Other interstate arrangements involve interstate compacts. Some of these are the result of federal mandates to cooperate on matters such as disposal of low-level radioactive waste, while others involve attempts to address interstate issues such as river basin management, regional economic development, bridges, extradition, education, conservation, energy, fires and fire prevention, driver's license reciprocal agreements, libraries, juvenile delinquents, pardons and paroles, pollution, flood control, and taxes.

Comparison to Other States

Forty-eight of the 50 states have governing authorities that operate like county government. They may be called parishes, boroughs, or counties, but they perform the same functions. Therefore, Arkansas is very much like the rest of the country in this structural feature.

Another way Arkansas counties are similar to those throughout the country is population size. According to the National Association of Counties, almost three-fourths of U.S. counties have populations under 50,000. Arkansas' rural character means the overwhelmingly majority of the state's counties are in this category.

A distinctive Arkansas county feature is administrative form. There are three basic forms of county government: commission; commission-administrator; and council-executive. A majority of counties are governed utilizing the commission form. In addition, several states give their counties the option to select their governing form. However, Arkansas is different, because the state legislature mandates that counties must be lead by an elected executive. While Arkansas counties may restructure and consolidate some county offices, they must preserve the county judge position.

Arkansas counties also have a financial advantage over many counties throughout the country. Only a slight majority of states allow counties to impose a sales tax. The state of Arkansas permits county governments to utilize this revenue source.

Arkansas is very much like the rest of the country with regard to municipal governments. For example, to incorporate or create a city, residents must petition the county or state for incorporation. One interesting feature in Arkansas is if a proposed new city is within five miles of a previously incorporated area, the older incorporated community must give their explicit permission to allow the new incorporated city.

Annexation is another feature that is common in most states. Historically, annexation was one of the most popular ways for cities to add territory and population. A key difference among the states is the level of difficulty concerning annexation. Some states make cities wait until landowners petition to be annexed into the city. These restrictions tend to make annexation very difficult. Other states make it very easy for cities to annex unincorporated areas. Arkansas rules seem to be somewhere between these two extremes. For example, individual votes cast to annex an area are weighted equally among those casting votes from the incorporated city as those cast from the proposed annexed area. This would tend to favor annexation efforts. However, other Arkansas procedures may serve to undermine annexation. As noted earlier, the community seeking annexation must provide a schedule of services that will be provided in the next three years. Therefore, annexation opponents can point to financial and taxation issues that will be affected by the additional territory.

Form of government is another way Arkansas is similar to other states. Most communities have mayor-council forms of government. As we have noted, this is by far the most common Arkansas municipal government structure. In addition, the numbers of city-manager governments have actually declined in Arkansas.

Finally, unique features of Arkansas local government are the progressive reforms of initiative, referendum, and recall. As noted in Chapter 2, only eighteen states allow the initiative and referendum procedures. Therefore, the citizen's ability to place local government issues like city government structure before the voters gives the Arkansas local electorate a great deal of power.

Historically, local governments focused only on vital services. Today, local governments are involved in economic development efforts, child welfare, water quality and numerous other issues. Arkansas local governments continue to be important agents addressing concerns of the state's citizenry.

Additional Resources

Arkansas Municipal League
http://www.arml.org/

Association of Arkansas Counties
http://www.arcounties.org/

Development Information Network of Arkansas
http://www.dina.org

Library of Congress - State Government Information
http://www.loc.gov/rr/news/stategov/stategov.html

The National Association of Counties
http://www.naco.org/

The U.S. Conference of Mayors
http://usmayors.org/

Political Parties and Interest Groups

Chapter 7

Political parties and interest groups are linkage institutions – mechanisms through which average citizens can convey their wishes to political officials. As such, they are considered two of the most important extra-governmental players in the political process.

Political Parties

Definition and Functions. Although there are varying definitions of political parties, one common feature is the concept of seeking elective office under a specific label. In addition, the individuals involved in party activities are seen as a loose-knit association of like-minded citizens. (Hershey, 2009: 6-7) It should be noted the party definition utilized in Arkansas focuses on actual or potential election activity. That is, a political party in Arkansas is defined by law as "any group of voters which, at the last preceding general election, polled for its candidate for governor in the state or nominees for presidential electors at least three percent of the entire vote cast for such office; or which files with the secretary of state a petition signed by qualified electors equal in number to at least three percent of the total vote cast for the office of governor or nominees for presidential electors at the last preceding election declaring their intention of organizing a political party..." (A.C.A. 7-1-101)

Moreover, any newly organized party in Arkansas will not be recognized or qualified to participate in elections until its officers state under oath that the party is not affiliated with the Communist party, does not advocate overthrow of the United States or state government, nor does it advocate sabotage or violence against the United States or state government. In addition, state law says that political parties shall have the right to prescribe the qualifications of their own membership, the qualifications for voting in their party primaries, and the right to establish rules and procedures for their own organization.

Although there is not complete agreement among analysts concerning political party functions, some of the most common

In This Chapter

Political Parties

Interest Groups

Comparison to Other States

Terms to Know

county committee (political party)

inside strategy (or direct lobbying)

interest groups

legal strategy (or litigation)

linkage institutions

outside strategy (or grassroots lobbying)

political party

state committee (political party)

roles associated with parties are recruiting candidates, contesting elections, encouraging participation, educating the public, and organizing opposition. (Hershey, 2009: 10) Parties attempt to recruit and screen potential individuals within the electoral process. From the White House to the courthouse, parties must find individuals who are willing to seek elective office under their label. Of course, there is a certain degree of self-recruitment involved for those vying for a major party nomination. That is, individuals must engage in activities and send signals that they are willing to pursue an electoral position. This is especially true for the most desirable posts such as U.S. Senator, U.S. Representative, or state constitutional officer. However, this can be a significant task for many local offices. When a city or county office provides little economic compensation or when effectively seeking the position requires resources almost equal to the salary, it is a challenge to recruit candidates. Moreover, due to long-term Democratic Party electoral dominance, one could argue a major task for the Arkansas Republican Party has been recruiting candidates.

Contesting elections is another role for political parties. This feature gives voters options when they make their election decisions. Parties are also involved in encouraging participation among the electorate. One way parties further citizen involvement is by engaging in voter registration drives. This makes potential voters eligible to take part in the political process. In addition, parties organize efforts to transport voters to the polls once they are registered to vote.

Another role of political parties is educating the public. Parties offer platforms providing their stance on many of the major political controversies. They also attempt to simplify the issues to assist average citizens in understanding these problems. Moreover, parties plan public meetings that give voters opportunities to express and hear various opinions on election or policy questions.

Finally, parties perform the role of loyal opposition. The idea is that parties keep each other honest. That is, when a party does not control the executive or legislative branch, they report the corrupt or deceptive practices of the party in power. In addition, the party out of power provides a tool for expressing dissatisfaction with the current policy decisions.

Party Organization. Political parties have decentralized organizations. Many analysts claim there are really fifty-one party organizations in the United States. One party organization exists at the national level, while each of the fifty states has a separate party structure. There is a great deal of diversity concerning the power and resources of the various state party apparatus. However, since a key feature of political parties is electoral activities, state and local organizations are important, because most elective positions are at these levels.

County Committees and County Conventions. Arkansas state parties follow the pattern of most states. The basic building blocks of the party structure are county committees. These committees are usually selected from precinct or wards, but the county committees provide the parties' basic working units. Each county party has an elected chair who heads the local organization. Just like state organizations, county committees vary in their strength and cohesiveness. Many county organizations do not operate year-round offices. That is, they only have official office space during election years. (Gibson et. al., 1985: 139-160) Therefore, it should come as no surprise that most county committees do not have any full-time staff members.

The county organizations are most viable during the election cycle. In Arkansas, they perform the political party functions discussed earlier. For example, county committees are involved in voter registration drives. In addition, county organizations coordinate efforts to provide citizens transportation to the polls on Election Day.

Moreover, county party organizations are involved in the presidential nomination process. County conventions or committees are involved in the process that selects individuals who will attend the National Party Convention, where the official party nominee for president is selected by party delegates.

State Committees and State Conventions. Historically in the U.S., the strongest party units were the state party organizations. Once again, states vary a great deal in the strength and enduring nature of their party organizations. Today, both the Democratic and Republican parties have ongoing formal party organizations. This was not always the case, because for many years the state party structures were merely nominal organizations. Each party has a state chairman and some paid staff members. The paid staff tends to expand during election years. The ongoing party business is usually conducted by an executive committee or central committee. Moreover, the parties usually take steps to provide geographic representation on the state committees through the use of U.S. congressional district boundaries. State committee meetings are held according to party rules. At the meetings, they conduct such business as they feel will benefit their party. Arkansas law requires that all political parties (this includes newly formed or third parties) hold state conventions following the biennial general primaries for the purpose of (1) "receiving, canvassing, and declaring the election results" and certifying the party nominees, and (2) performing such other duties as may be required by party rules or by law. One "other such duty" is the election of members of the state committee. (A.C.A. 7-3-107)

Another interesting party feature is the determination of majority or minority party status. Arkansas law defines the majority party as that political party whose candidates were elected to a majority of the seven constitutional offices of the state in the last general election. The minority party is that party whose candidates were elected to less than a majority of the constitutional officers in the last general election or the political party which polled the second greatest number of votes for governor if all elected constitutional officers were of the same party. (A.C.A. 7-1-101)

National, State, and County Committee Members. One additional political party function in the U.S. is the selection of various national, state and county committees. Those selected as national committee members of the political parties are chosen in the manner prescribed by party rules. These vary somewhat between the two political parties. For example, the Democratic Party takes steps to insure gender equity for national committee service. The Republican Party may encourage this activity, but the rules are not as explicit on these matters. State committee members are elected by the respective state county conventions and approved by the respective state conventions. The law provides that those voting in the party primaries shall elect county committee members from each election precinct, township, or city ward. In practice, however, both parties do not hold primaries in all counties and often there are insufficient qualified candidates running to fill all committee vacancies. In such cases, committee members may be selected to fill these positions at any public meeting of the county committee.

Overall, Arkansas parties perform the political functions expected of these organizations. There are states with stronger and more cohesive parties, but the state's major parties seem to be taking steps to increase their organizational vitality.

Interest Groups

Interest groups link like-minded citizens and institutions with governmental decision-makers. An interest group can be defined as "any association of like-minded citizens that have some shared attitude, opinion, or value; who make demands on others in society, with respect to that shared attitude, opinion, or value." This definition involves two important characteristics. First, interest group members must have something in common. This can be real or imagined, but they must see themselves as part of a group. In addition, interest groups must make demands on others in society. It is not enough to think like others or to have a common value. Interest group members must take the next step and act on their joint concerns. Our discussion now turns to the various types of interest groups, the nature of interest group resources, and the strategies groups utilize to influence government policies.

Types of Interest Groups. There are a wide variety of interest groups in the U.S. and in the state of Arkansas. One common type is the economic interest group. Economic interest groups participate in the political process in order to provide monetary or economic benefits to their members. Some of the groups' goals may include additional or reduced governmental regulation, direct subsidies, or lower taxes. This is the most common type of interest group. Examples of economic groups would be the Farm Bureau, the banking industry, and public utilities.

Another group type focuses on the concept of equal opportunity. These groups are interested in racial, gender, and age equality. They tend to be ideological, but they may attempt to build alliances across differing political viewpoints. Equal opportunity groups include the National Association for the Advancement of Colored People (NAACP), the National Organization for Women (NOW), and the American Association of Retired Persons (AARP).

Public interest groups also play a vital role in the political arena. These groups are distinctive, because they seek benefits that extend beyond their members. Their goal is to benefit the general public, not just individuals who belong to the group. Examples of public interest groups would be the League of Women Voters, Common Cause, Arkansas Education Association, consumer groups, and religious groups. Critics of public interest groups accept the fact that these groups do what they consider best for the general public. However, they emphasize that the group is doing what it considers to be best for the general public. However, not everyone agrees that what they promote is in the public's best interest. An example is clear-cutting in national forests. There may be many citizens who disagree with this perspective and do not think this policy is in the public interest.

Other interest groups focus on single issues. For example, abortion (NARAL Pro-Choice America and National Right to Life) and gun ownership (Coalition to Stop Gun Violence and National Rifle Association) are two polarizing issues that generate substantial debate.

Interest Group Resources. Interest groups have a variety of resources that can assist them in their political efforts. An effective group is not required to have all of these assets. However, the more tools they have available, the more likely they will be successful in their policy pursuits. One group resource is the intensity of its members. Groups whose members are in strong agreement with the organization's goals have a major advantage over those bodies where members only nominally identify with the association. The more readily group members identify with the group's mission, the more likely they are to devote time, energy and money to achieve these objectives. They will make telephone calls and write letters or emails to political decision-makers. In addition, they are willing to make contributions to the candidates who support the group's political goals.

Size of membership is also considered an interest group resource. However, not all analysts agree what size is optimal for group influence. Some argue that large memberships provide obvious benefits. With many supporters, the organization may have members throughout the state. This can be translated into potential contacts with every member of the legislature. However, there are those who argue that small groups tend to be the most effective. The basic contention is that small groups are more cohesive. Most importantly, fewer members mean whatever benefits are received by the group, the rewards are bigger for each individual. That is, the goods are divided among less people, so each individual receives a greater share. (Olson, 1965: 33-34)

Quality leadership is another characteristic that can assist interest groups in their political efforts. Effective leaders can reduce in-fighting among the members. In addition, they can keep the organization on track and working toward the same objectives. Moreover, average members may not be able to match the expertise or contacts of the leader.

Finally, financial resources are key because money can be translated into other resources. For example, if the group needs a quality leader, a wealthy organization can hire a leader with the desired skills. In addition, financial status tends to give the group easier access to many decision-making arenas. Although there is no single answer to what makes an interest group politically successful, this resource list provides a good starting point for interested citizens. By evaluating these assets, one can begin to see some of the factors that lead to interest group success.

Strategies and Tactics of Interest Groups. In general, interest groups may pursue three major strategies to influence or lobby political decision makers.

Inside Strategy or Direct Lobbying. The first of these approaches can be described as an inside strategy, where the group engages in direct contact with government officials. There are various ways that interest groups can engage in these direct tactics. One obvious technique is meeting with officials to discuss issues of concern to the group. This approach allows group representatives to present their objectives to the decision-maker. Another element of direct lobbying is providing information to public authorities. Many times interest groups may have knowledge that is unavailable through other sources. Moreover, groups can lobby by testifying before legislative committee hearings. In fact, some interest groups may be actively involved in drafting state legislative proposals. These actions provide additional ways for groups to communicate their wishes to government actors.

Often associated with direct lobbying is entertainment, where group representatives pay for meals and provide other benefits to public officials. Groups may also make campaign contributions, provide campaign volunteers, or sponsor fundraising opportunities for favored candidates. The goal is to influence who holds office, thus creating a sympathetic environment for the organization's objectives. Whatever direct techniques are utilized, they have the advantage of precise communication with the public official. Thus there is a reduced chance of miscommunication and less potential for confusion about the group's desires. Generally, direct lobbying or an inside strategy is the most effective way for interest groups to influence the political process.

Outside Strategy or Grassroots Lobbying. Grassroots mobilization works at shaping public opinion so average citizens are responsive to an interest group's goals. The focus of this type of lobbying is involving average citizens in the policy making process. Of course if this tactic is going to be successful, it is essential that average citizens are stimulated to be involved in the policy-making process. Interest groups generate awareness and encourage citizen involvement through advertising and Internet-based technologies. Ultimately, the group needs citizens to contact decision-makers and promote the organization's perspectives.

The outside strategy seeks to make elected officials more receptive to constituents. To accomplish the, an outside strategy uses constituents as lobbyists. This may be a so-called "shotgun" approach, where the interest groups seeks to have a large numbers of citizens act together by writing or phoning a legislator or executive official. The group can attempt a "rifle" approach when relying on public involvement. In the "rifle" approach, the group has an influential constituent contact a legislator or executive leader on a specific issue. The assumption is the influential individual may have access that has been denied the group. Although direct lobbying is believed to be the most effective tactic to influence legislation, some research has indicated that Arkansas decision-makers are responsive to the public as amateur lobbyists. (Whistler and Dunn, 1987: 38-39) Overall, the part-time citizen legislature seems to create an environment where citizens can impact Arkansas' governmental process.

Legal Strategy or Litigation. A legal strategy means that interest groups are using the court system to pursue their policy goals. This has become a more popular approach because courts are playing a more active role in government decisions. Arkansas is no exception. The Lake View School District case (see Chapter 9), for example, has changed the way the state finances public education. Since education spending is the largest single item in the state's budget, this ruling and others continue to shape state politics.

When a group employs a legal strategy, it may be a direct party in the litigation. The group may provide legal arguments to support one side in a case. It can also initiate a class action lawsuit. In this situation, the group brings a suit on behalf of individuals with a shared characteristic that makes them a legal class. It can provide legal staff or spend monies to pay attorneys who are arguing the case. Also, the group can participate in litigation where the group is not a direct party in the suit.

Interest groups may submit *amicus curiae* ("Friend of the Court") briefs. This means the group provides a legal rationale for deciding a case in accordance with the group's views. Overall, these three strategies can all be effective techniques to influence state governmental decision-making.

Comparison to Other States

As with most southern states, the Democratic Party has been the predominant party in Arkansas, and most of those holding elective positions in the state legislature and in county governments are Democrats. In fact, those claiming Democratic Party affiliation have held the majority of seats in the General Assembly for over one hundred years. For much of the 20th century, the South was referred to as the "Solid South," indicating a high degree of loyalty to Democratic candidates for any elective office. Even though Republicans have increased their number of seats in the General Assembly, Democrats continue to be the majority party. In neighboring states, however, Republicans have made significant gains in state legislative races.

Some change seems to be occurring in Arkansas' voting patterns in presidential elections. Since the 1970s, only two Democratic presidential candidates from the South have been victorious in Arkansas (Jimmy Carter in 1976 and Bill Clinton in 1992 and 1996). In all other presidential elections, Arkansans have cast more votes for the Republican presidential candidate (1972, 1980, 1984, 1988, 2000, 2004, and 2008).

Examining the vote totals and victory margins for Democratic Party candidates seeking what might be considered lesser constitutional offices (e.g., State Auditor and Land Commissioner) is also illuminating. In these races, where name recognition is much lower and political advertising is limited, Democratic nominees have consistently outpolled their Republican opponents. This indicates that the Democratic Party label remains a reliable predictor of who wins in down-ballot contests.

Finally, most states in the "Solid South" have begun to elect more Republicans to national offices. The partisan identification of the U.S. Senators representing Arkansas' bordering states is overwhelmingly Republican. For a time, both U.S. senators from Texas, Oklahoma, Missouri, Tennessee and Mississippi were Republicans, while Louisiana had one Republican senator. Only Arkansas has maintained the traditional U.S. Senate delegation of two Democrats. Again, partisan change is occurring in Arkansas but more slowly than in the rest of the region. One reason is Arkansas' low socioeconomic status. Another is less suburban growth.

Historically, the South has had weak political party organizations. This characteristic has provided interest groups an opportunity to expand their political influence in the state. Clive Thomas and Ronald Hrebenar have identified five basic categories for interest group influence within the states. These categories are dominant, dominant complementary, complementary, complementary subordinate, and subordinate. The dominant category means that interest groups have a consistent and guiding impact on state decision-making. Those states in the dominant complementary category are areas where interest groups have a great deal of power, but they are sometimes balanced by other political actors. The complementary category is one where there is equilibrium between the influence of interest groups and other state institutions. The complementary subordinate means interest groups may have some impact, but other political leaders play a greater policy role. Subordinate describes a situation where interest groups are weak and ineffective in the governmental arena. Thomas and Hrebenar found no states fit into the subordinate category. Arkansas, along with 25 other states, was classified as dominant complementary. (Thomas and Hrebenar, 1999: 13) This indicates that interest group influence in Arkansas is similar to many other states. Moreover, it indicates that interest groups can have a significant effect on state government.

There are a number of Arkansas features that contribute to the impact of interest groups. One factor that seems to empower interest groups is a decentralized state executive. A variety of constitutional officers provide many points of access and influence. In addition, the citizen legislature remains in close touch with the public. This easier access can lead to expanded opportunities for political lobbying. Also, as noted earlier, Arkansas' political parties have traditionally been weak, which allows greater group influence.

Citizens may want to know what associations are considered the state's most influential groups. Research by Donald Whistler and Charles Dunn in the early 1980s indicated that the following organizations were considered the most powerful. These groups were the Arkansas Education Association (AEA), the Farm Bureau, financial institutions, utilities, and the state highway commission. Whistler and Dunn obtained their results from a survey of professional lobbyists and state legislators. (Whistler and Dunn, 1987: 30-31) Although the state has changed over the last two decades, these groups still seem to be key political players in the state.

Interest groups in Arkansas are in a state of flux. The state may be in the dominant complementary category for interest group influence, but this is not a permanent situation. If the state's economy continues to diversify, this should lead to the creation of additional interests. With new interests entering the political arena, old alliances may be challenged. Therefore, citizens should remain attentive to the evolving nature of political party rivalries and interest group competition.

Additional Resources

Arkansas Democratic Party
http://www.arkdems.org/index.php

Arkansas Republican Party
http://www.arkansasgop.org/

Democratic National Committee
http://www.democrats.org/

Republican National Committee
http://www.rnc.org/

Elections

Chapter 8

Voting is an important feature in democratic societies. Free and open elections allow citizens to choose their decision makers. Moreover, elections provide legitimacy for public officials, because this process formally establishes the "consent of the governed" concerning their actions. As in any electoral system, the current rules and procedures have developed over a long period of time. Many changes are the result of addressing past shortcomings in the electoral process. New circumstances continue to require adjustments and changes in election procedures.

Voting Rules

The original intent of the United States Constitution was to leave matters regarding elections and voter qualifications to the states. However, amendments to the constitution, decisions made by the United States Supreme Court, and federal laws have placed some restrictions on the states' powers in regard to the election process.

United States Constitutional Amendments Regarding the Right to Vote		
Amendment	Year Passed	Reason Right to Vote Cannot Be Denied
XV	1870	"race, color, or previous condition of servitude"
XIX	1920	"on account of sex"
XXIV	1964	"failure to pay any poll tax or other tax"
XXVI	1971	"any citizen 18 years of age or older"

In recent years, the United States Supreme Court has consistently interpreted the Fourteenth Amendment guaranteeing "equal protection of the laws" to mean that the states must apportion their representative districts to be of equal population size so that each citizen's vote will be of equal value to every other

In This Chapter

Voting Rules

Voter Registration

Elections

Candidates

Comparison to Other States

Terms to Know

absentee voting

early voting

independent candidates

general elections

party nominees

primaries

presidential preferential primaries

suffrage

write-ins

95

citizen's vote. It has also struck down lengthy residence requirements as a prerequisite for voting, declaring that such deny equal suffrage to all citizens. The Voting Rights Acts of 1965, 1970, 1982 and 1988 specifically spelled out the meaning of equal suffrage and thereby helped make voting and election laws considerably more uniform throughout the nation. In addition, the passage of the National Voter Registration Act, or the "Motor Voter" Act, required that states allow simultaneous application for driver's licenses and voter registration. It should be noted that voters must still complete the application materials. The legislation facilitates easier voter registration, but it does not provide automatic voter registration with driver's license renewal.

The Arkansas Constitution guarantees that "elections shall be free and equal. No power, civil or military, shall ever interfere to prevent the free exercise of the right of suffrage..." (Article III, Section 2). Seven subsequent amendments to the constitution and numerous laws have detailed voter registration and election procedures, but it was not until 1967 that the election procedures were compiled into a usable code. However, there is still considerable confusion about election laws, and election law revision is addressed by almost every General Assembly. Fundamentally, the detailed rules of election procedures require continual oversight.

Voter Registration

Eligibility. To be eligible to vote in Arkansas, a person must be a citizen of the United States, 18 years of age, and have registered to vote with the permanent registrar (county clerk) of the county where that person lives. There are no lengths of residence requirements, although a citizen must register at least 30 days before an election and must have resided at the location listed on the registration affidavit 31 calendar days prior to the election.

Registration. Numerous changes have been made in the voter registration system in Arkansas to make it comply with the Motor Voter Act. In addition to the permanent registrar (county clerk), the following may now serve as voter registration agencies: the Office of Driver Service of the Revenue Division; public assistance agencies; disabilities agencies; public libraries; and the Arkansas National Guard. To register, a prospective voter must go in person to the county clerk's office or to one of these agencies. The law allows county clerks to assign deputy registrars at polling places on election day, although it does not grant those registering the right to vote in that day's election. A person who is ill or disabled shall be registered by the permanent registrar or deputy "at his place of abode within such county, if practicable..." Members of the armed forces while in active service, members of the Merchant

Marine, citizens of Arkansas residing temporarily outside the territorial limits of the United States and their "spouses and dependents when residing with or accompanying them" need not register to vote.

Once a voter is registered, it is not necessary to register again unless the registration is canceled. Periodically, counties will mail notices to voters who have not voted in several elections in order to update voter rolls. If a voter receives such a notice, it is important to mark the correct address and return the card to the county clerk so the voter registration can be updated. Cancellation occurs when a voter:
- changes residence to an address outside the county;
- dies or changes his or her name;
- has been convicted of a felony and has not discharged the sentence; or
- is not a lawfully qualified or registered elector of the state or county

County clerks are required to notify voters 30 days before canceling their registration. This may be done by mail or by publication of the list of names of those whose registration is to be canceled in a newspaper of general circulation in the county. Voters so informed may re-establish their registration by notifying the county clerk of their desire to remain registered. A voter who does not notify the county clerk must register again. A change of address within the county may be corrected in person or by signing a mailed request giving the old and new addresses. In case of a change of county or of name, a person must register again in person. In Arkansas, people do not declare their political party affiliation when they register.

Elections

Administration. The responsibility for administration of existing Arkansas election laws is shared by the State Board of Election Commissioners, the auditor of state (for voter registration), and the secretary of state (elections). In actual practice, primary responsibility for voter registration rests with the 75 permanent registrars (county clerks), and for elections with the 75 County Boards of Election Commissioners.

The State Board of Election Commissioners consists of seven persons with at least one from each congressional district. The members are: the secretary of state, one person designated by the Democratic Party, one by the Republican Party, one chosen by the president pro tem of the Senate, one chosen by the speaker of the House, and two by the governor. When selecting election commissioners, the governor must select one person who is a county clerk, and one person who has served as a county election commissioner for at least three years. Except for the secretary of state and the county clerk, no member shall be an elected officer. The secretary of state serves as chair and keeps the board's meeting records. The board is required to meet at least every three months.

A duty of the State Board of Election Commissioners is to choose one member of county election commissions. The board also inspects and approves (or disapproves) the different types of voting machines or electronic voting systems to ensure compliance with the standards established by law. The board may perform additional duties such as publishing of an election handbook, conducting statewide training for election judges and clerks, investigating citizen complaints, and establishing guidelines for and monitoring the qualifications of election officials. Overall, state law requires the State Board of Election Commissioners to "formulate, adopt and promulgate all necessary rules and regulations to assure even and consistent application of fair and orderly election procedures." (A.C.A. 7-4-101)

The County Boards of Election Commissioners are responsible for the administration of elections in their respective counties. Historically, party primaries were the responsibility of the political parties, but now state law provides that the cost of party primaries will be paid for by the state. The County Boards are composed of three individuals: the chairs of the county majority and minority parties and a third member selected by the State Board of Election Commissioners from a list of five names submitted by the county committee of the majority party. Elected officials may not serve on this board. If a county party chair chooses not to serve, a substitute may be designated.

The County Board of Election Commissioners is charged with apportionment of the county into quorum court districts and with management of elections. Regarding elections, the county board is responsible for:
- establishing voting precinct boundaries;
- choosing polling places, which must be accessible to the disabled;
- selecting election judges, clerks, and election sheriffs to oversee the election process;
- organizing training for election officials to ensure that at least one official at every polling site has been trained;
- printing the ballots;
- providing voter lists, tally sheets, certificates, and ballot boxes;
- providing voter booths if voting machines are not used;
- advising the quorum court on use and purchase of voting machines or voting devices; and
- counting, certifying, and reporting election results.

All polls must open by 7:30 a.m. and close at 7:30 p.m. Every polling site in the state offers at least one touch-screen voting machine that is accessible for voters with physical and visual disabilities. Some sites offer paper ballots that are counted electronically. The system used is determined by the County Board of Election Commissioners, but it must be a system approved by the State Board of Election Commissioners. The constitution and state laws are written primarily to cover use of paper ballots and voting machines. However, because of the variety of new systems now available, state laws do not always cover all election circumstances. Each polling site must have a minimum of two election clerks, one election judge, and one election sheriff.

In elections where paper ballots are used, the County Board of Election Commissioners, or in a primary election, the county political party committee, is responsible for appointing a "sufficient number of judges and clerks at each ballot box." However, each voting precinct must have at least one set of three judges and two clerks and one election sheriff. The law provides that election judges and clerks may work split or half-day shifts if the county board of elections approves. Where paper ballots are used, the election commission is responsible for providing voting booths which are "situated so as to permit voters to prepare their ballots screened from observation."

In a county where voting machines or electronic voting systems are used, the County Board of Election Commissioners must appoint one judge and one clerk to represent each of the majority or minority parties and one election sheriff. Additional sets of judges and clerks may be appointed if it is determined that they are necessary.

All election officials must take an oath swearing that they will perform their duties to the best of their abilities and that they will "studiously endeavor to prevent fraud, deceit and abuse," and that they will not disclose how any voter voted. In case no person authorized to administer oaths is present at the opening of an election, judges may administer the oath to each other and to the clerks.

By state law, every employer must schedule work hours of employees on election days to assure that every employee will have the opportunity to vote. An employer failing to do so may be fined not less than $25 or more than $250. (A.C.A. 7-1-102)

Absentee Voting. Any qualified elector may vote absentee. It is necessary for a voter to declare that he or she would be "unavoidably absent" on the day of election or would be unable to attend due to illness or physical disability. The county clerk is custodian of all absentee ballots and administrator of absentee voting procedures. To vote absentee, a voter must first request a ballot. Applications for absentee ballots must be signed by the applicant or, if sent by facsimile machine, must bear a verifiable facsimile of the applicant's signature.

Applications for absentee voting may be secured by:
- requesting by mail or from the county clerk's office an application form. The application form must be signed by the voter and returned to the county clerk's office in one of four ways:
    - in person at the county clerk's office;
    - by mail from 90 days to one day before the election;
    - by delivery of the application form to the office of the county clerk by any immediate relative;
    - by delivery of the application form to the office of the county clerk by 1:30 on election day or by the administrative head of a hospital or nursing home.
- sending a signed postcard or letter to the county clerk requesting a ballot at least seven calendar days prior to the election.
- requesting by facsimile machine an application from the county clerk's office and then transmitting the completed application by facsimile to that office within the time limits specified.

Upon receipt of the application form or the mailed request, the county clerk must determine that the signature is identical with the one on the voter's registration affidavit. Then the county clerk will give the voter a ballot, mail a ballot to the voter, or give a ballot to an immediate relative or hospital agent. Delivery of absentee ballots by relatives or hospital agents is limited to five per person. Completed ballots may be returned by the voter to the county clerk's office no later than the day before the election; or they may be mailed to the county clerk, but must be received not later than 7:30 p.m. the day of the election; or be delivered to the county clerk's office by a close relative or hospital agent by 7:30 p.m. the day of the election.

Any person eligible to vote by absentee ballot may request the county clerk to mail to an address within the continental United States an application for an absentee ballot for an election and for each election thereafter. The request remains in effect for one year unless revoked by the voter. Also, citizens of the United States temporarily residing outside the United States, and their spouses and dependents may request absentee ballots for any one or more elections during any one calendar year by submitting only one application. In both cases, absentee ballots are mailed automatically by the county clerk no later than 30 days prior to each election.

To assure that all overseas ballots will be counted, the law requires County Boards of Election Commissioners to begin the certification process no earlier than 48 hours nor later than ten calendar days after an election. The process must be complete within 14 days. The County Board of Election Commissioners is responsible for delivering the ballots to the county clerk at least 25 days before an election so that there will be adequate time for mailing ballots. (A.C.A. 7-5-701)

Early Voting. A recent initiative that assists Arkansas voters is the practice of early voting. Citizens may take advantage of early voting 15 days before an election. In smaller counties (population less than 150,000), early voting takes place at county clerk offices. County election boards in larger counties (population of 150,000 or more) may opt to hold early voting at additional polling places. In this case, the county clerk must inform the public about these other locations. In most situations, early voting occurs during the regular office hours of the county clerk; however, a county's election board may extend the office hours to accommodate early voting. (A.C.A. 7-5-418)

Cost of Elections. Costs of all elections are the responsibility of the county operating through the County Board of Election Commissioners. However, cities and incorporated towns must reimburse the board for expenses of general elections in "an amount equal to a figure derived by multiplying 50% of the total cost of the election by a fraction, the numerator of which shall be number of voters from the city or town casting ballots in the election and the denominator of which shall be the total number of voters casting ballots in the election." In elections where city, town, or school districts have races, questions, or issues on the ballot, those entities reimburse the county for total cost of their elections or for that portion of the cost created by the inclusion of their items on the ballot.

Primary elections are the responsibility of the state. The General Assembly appropriates primary election funds to the State Board of Election Commissioners. Within each county, the county board of election commissioners conducts political party primary elections under the direction of the state board.

Judges, clerks, and sheriffs serving at elections are paid varying amounts, depending on the level set by the quorum court. The quorum court must also appropriate funds for printing of ballots; purchase, storage and care of equipment; and for preparing and transporting voting machines and electronic voting systems.

Election Law Violations. Some election offenses are classified as Class-A misdemeanors and are punishable by a fine not exceeding $1,000 or by imprisonment in the penitentiary not exceeding one year, or by both. Any person convicted of any of these offenses is ineligible to hold office or employment in any department of the state. An employee of the state convicted of one of these offenses is immediately removed from employment. If any person is convicted of a violation while holding public office, the action "shall be deemed a misfeasance and malfeasance in office and shall subject the person to impeachment."

Violating any of the following rules constitutes a Class-A misdemeanor (A.C.A. 7-1-103):

- No article, statement or communication appearing in any newspaper intended or calculated to influence the vote of any elector in any election and for which money is paid may be printed without being preceded by or followed by the phrase "Paid Political Advertisement" in conspicuous letters.
- No person may assess, solicit, or coerce a state employee into making a contribution for a political purpose.
- Public officers may not use any public room or office as political headquarters or as distribution center for campaign materials.
- No campaign banners, cards, or campaign literature may be placed on any cars, trucks, or tractors belonging to the state of Arkansas or any municipality or county in the state.
- No electioneering may be done within 100 feet of a polling place during the early voting period or on Election Day.
- No person shall make a bet or wager on the result of any election.
- No election official shall perform his duties without taking the prescribed oath.
- No election results shall be divulged until at least 30 minutes after the closing of the polls.

Other violations are listed as Class-D felonies and are punishable by not less than one year or more than five years in the state penitentiary or a fine not to exceed $5,000 or both. Violating any of the following rules constitutes a Class-D felony (A.C.A. 7-1-104):

- No election official shall fraudulently permit another person to vote illegally.
- No election official shall willfully make a false count of any election ballots.
- No public official responsible for registration shall forge a registration or allow a person not entitled to register to do so.
- No person shall vote more than once in any election.
- No person shall tamper with a voting machine or attempt to affect the results.

Primaries. The political parties choose their nominees for national, state, and local offices through the primary elections. Primaries must be conducted in conformity with Arkansas law. The preferential primary is held three weeks before the general primary. The general primary need not be held if all winners receive a majority of the votes cast in the preferential primary. However, in those races where there were three or more candidates and no one received a majority of the votes, a general primary must be held. Usually, the general primary is held the second Tuesday in June, but primary dates have been changed by legislative action in order to meet deadlines for election of delegates to the national conventions. The state is responsible for the cost of primary elections, whereas the administration of them is the responsibility of the State Board of Election Commissioners. The parties determine the qualifications of candidates seeking the party nomination. Because the state pays for primaries, common polling places or joint primaries are used for the primary elections of both parties.

Since Arkansas voters do not need to declare their party affiliation when they register to vote, they may vote in either primary. However, a person who votes in the preferential primary of one party may not vote in the general primary of the other party.

Presidential Preferential Primaries. Each presidential election year, national parties specify how many delegates each state will be allowed to send to their national party conventions. Although there are a variety of methods for choosing delegates, Arkansas requires parties to use a presidential preferential primary. Citizens may choose to vote in one party's primary. The result of the primary determines how many Arkansas delegates presidential candidates will have at the national convention. The state committees of the respective political parties then choose their delegates to the national nominating convention in proportion to the votes cast for the various presidential candidates. (A.C.A. 7-8-201) Consider this example. Assume that in the upcoming presidential election, Arkansas is allocated 40 delegates to the Democratic National Party Convention. Democratic presidential Candidate A receives 40% of the vote in the primary, while Candidate B gets 30%, Candidate C earns 20%, and Candidate D has 10%. Therefore, Arkansas' Democratic delegates would be allocated as follows: Candidate A would have 16 delegates; Candidate B would get 12 delegates; Candidate C would receive 8 delegates; and Candidate D would have 4 delegates.

Arkansas Elections		
Type	Purpose	Date
GENERAL ELECTIONS		
General Elections	U.S., State, County, and Municipal Offices; Ballot Issues and Constitutional Amendments	1st Tuesday following 1st Monday in November
School Elections	School Board members; millage elections	3rd Tuesday in September
Special Elections	Issues, fill vacancies, run-offs; tie votes; referenda	Set by governor, county, or municipal ordinance
PARTY PRIMARIES		
Preferential Primary	County committees, and nominees for state and local offices	2 weeks before party general primary (set by state law and parties)
General Primary	Run-offs for those who did not receive majority vote in preferential primary	2nd Tuesday in June (set by state law and parties)
Municipal Primary	Municipal officers	6th Tuesday before General Election if requested by city or town government
Preferential Presidential Primary	Nominees for U.S. President and Vice President	Set by state law
Special Primary	Fill a vacancy in office of lieutenant governor, member of U.S. House or General Assembly	Set by governor if parties want a primary
Source: League of Women Voters of Arkansas		

Candidates

Party Nominees. To run for election as a party's nominee, a person must file any pledge required by the political party and pay such ballot fees as required by the party. The candidate must also sign the political practices pledge, which is filed with the secretary of state for national and state offices and with the county clerk for local offices. The filing shall be done during "regular office hours not earlier than 12:00 noon on the third Tuesday in March and ending at 12:00 noon on the fourteenth day thereafter before the preferential primary election." (A.C.A. 7-7-203)

The ballot fees required by the parties are used for managing party affairs. The state political party committees set the filing fees for those running for U.S. Congress and for state office. Ballot fees for local officials vary widely from county to county. However, the constitutionality of ballot fees, especially when they are so large that they discourage some people from running for office, has been challenged in the courts on several occasions.

As a result of these challenges, alternate systems of filing are provided by the political parties, including filing by petition under the rules established for filing by the political parties and approved by the federal courts.

Should a party nominee die or withdraw from a race before the election, the vacancy created may be filled by certification of the chairman and secretary of any convention of delegates or by a special primary election. The governor must be notified within five days and informed whether the party chooses to fill the vacancy by an election or by convention. If the party fails to inform the governor within the five-day period, the nomination vacancy is not filled. This means the party is denied a formal representative in that election. (A.C.A. 7-7-104)

Independents. Independents may also file for office, but since they do not run in the party primaries, they file for ballot position in the general election. The deadline for filing as an independent is the date set for party candidates to sign their political practices pledge or May 1, whichever is later. To run as an independent for state office or for the United States Congress, a candidate must file a petition signed by at least three percent of the qualified voters, although never more than 10,000 signatures, whichever is less. To run as an independent for county, township or district office, the candidate must file a petition signed by at least three percent, though never more than 2,000, of the qualified electors in the county, township, or district in which the person is seeking office. Independent candidates filing for municipal office may qualify by filing a petition containing the signatures of not less than ten electors for incorporated towns and second class cities, and not fewer than 30 electors for first class cities. A person who has been defeated in a party primary is not permitted to file as an independent in the general election for the office for which that candidate was defeated in the primary. (A.C.A. 7-7-103)

Write-Ins. Provision is made for write-in candidates on general election ballots. To qualify as a write-in candidate, that person must have filed his or her intention to be a write-in candidate at least 90 days prior to the election. (A.C.A. 7-5-205)

Political Practices Act. All candidates for state, county, municipal, or township offices must sign a political practices pledge, which states that the candidate is familiar with the political practices requirements and "will, in good faith, comply with their terms." They must also certify that they "have never been convicted of a felony in Arkansas or in any other jurisdiction outside of Arkansas." Candidates must sign that they are not members of communist or subversive parties. The pledge also includes a promise to avoid election violations, whether they are misdemeanors or felonies. (A.C.A. 7-6-102)

Campaign Financing. Arkansas' campaign finance laws require candidates to file financial disclosure statements. In addition, they regulate the financial activity of political actions committees (PACs), candidate exploratory committees, ballot question initiatives, and the candidates themselves. PACs, private groups organized to elect political candidates, are required to register and file reports with the secretary of state. Most PACs are also limited to accepting contributions of a maximum of $200 per person per year and to contributing more than $1,000 per candidate per election. In addition, they must file reports with the secretary of state not more than 15 days after the end of the month. However, Arkansas has created a special category for "small donor" political action committees. These PACs may not accept contributions of more than $25 from any contributor. Because they handle smaller financial resources, they file quarterly reports.

Any person in Arkansas considering whether to run for state public office may register with the secretary of state the formation of an "exploratory" committee. If a committee is formed, it must register within 15 days after receipt of contributions. When a candidate enters the race, the exploratory committee must disband and transfer the funds to the candidate. All candidates for public office in Arkansas must file Campaign Contribution and Expenditure Reports. Candidates for state and district offices and for most county and municipal offices must also file Statements of Financial Interest. Candidates for school board and some county and municipal boards and commissions must file the Code of Ethics. On the Campaign Contribution and Expenditure Report, a candidate must report carryover from any past campaigns, names and addresses of all persons making contributions of $100 or more, description of non-money items received, itemization of all expenditures which exceeded $100, loans made, and a final report of campaign surplus or debt. Cash or anonymous contributions of over $100 and cash expenditures of over $50 are prohibited. All contributions of over $1,000 per election are prohibited except that there is no limitation on a candidate's own contributions. State constitutional officers and members of the House and Senate are prohibited from accepting contributions during the period of 30 days before and 30 days after any regular session of the General Assembly. Pre-election reports are required of all candidates except those unopposed and those who have received total contributions of less than $500. All candidates must file a final report of contributions and expenditures by categories within 30 days after the election. The Arkansas Ethics Commission is given the authority to enforce these campaign finance regulations. (A.C.A. 7-6-203, 7-6-204, and 7-6-216)

Ballot question committees and legislative question committees are also regulated and must report their contributions and expenditures. Ballot question committees are defined as "any person, located within or outside Arkansas, who receives contributions, who makes expenditures for the purpose of expressly advocating the qualification, passage, or defeat of any ballot question." Such committees must file statements of organization within fifteen days of their organization and must also file financial disclosure statements listing all contributors and expenditures of $100 or more, if more than two percent of their budget is expended on a ballot issue or the group spends $10,000 or more on a ballot issue. (A.C.A. 7-9-402 and 7-9-404) Both statements are filed with the Arkansas Ethics Commission, which also has the authority to enforce legislation involving the issue committees.

Comparison to Other States

Many of the characteristics of Arkansas' electoral process are very similar to other states. In most states, the secretary of state is the chief elections officer, and states tend to rely upon some type of state board of elections. Since voting is a local process, local officials have a significant role in conducting elections. Local personnel take the lead in registering citizens to vote, selecting polling places, and serving as Election Day workers. Therefore, the nuts-and-bolts of this important democratic process happen at the grassroots level.

Arkansas does have some distinctive voting processes. One of these unique features is general (runoff) primaries. Only nine states rely upon the runoff process to select party nominees. The goal of a runoff is to insure that the candidate who receives the party nomination obtains majority vote approval. Runoffs can only occur when three or more candidates are seeking the party label. As noted earlier, if no candidate receives a majority vote in the preferential primary, the two individuals who receive the most votes face each other in the runoff.

Supporters of the runoff primary contend that it ensures the party nominee has the support of most party voters. Consider the following example. In a state that does not have a runoff system, ten candidates are seeking the party nomination. The leading candidate receives 20% of the vote, which automatically makes this person the party nominee. Runoff advocates in this case would point out that 80% of the primary voters did not select this candidate. Therefore, a runoff can more accurately reflect the will of the party majority.

Critics of the runoff system focus on two potential problems. One concern is the runoff process weakens the party's nominee in the general election. When party members compete against each other in two electoral contests, divisiveness within the party may increase. Another concern is expressed by minority candidates. These candidates note they can receive more votes than their fellow partisans in the initial primary electoral process. However, they are disadvantaged when the race is narrowed to only two potential party nominees. So far, Arkansas officials continue to endorse the use of the runoff electoral system.

Another important change in Arkansas elections is the development of early voting. Historically, absentee balloting required voters to provide information that they would be unable to vote on Election Day. Early voting does not place these restrictions on voters. Since early voting is available fifteen days before an election, this expands the opportunities for citizens to participate in the electoral process. One goal of the electoral system is to make changes that increase voter participation, and early voting can assist in this effort.

Concern over the role of money in campaigns has also been addressed by Arkansas' legislators. Now, campaign finance regulations place limits on campaign contributions. In addition, the rules require periodic reporting of campaign contributions and expenditures by most federal, state, and local office holders. The state also created the Ethics Commission to serve as an independent body to enforce campaign finance guidelines.

As the 2000 Presidential Election demonstrated, the election process can be complex and full of potential pitfalls. Arkansas continues to work to improve its election procedures as required by the Federal Help America Vote Act. Steps have been taken to increase the secrecy of ballots and expand citizens' opportunities to participate in the political system. There is a consensus that elections are important in any democratic society. Therefore, the electoral process continues to undergo scrutiny and reform as efforts are made to encourage citizen involvement.

Additional Resources

Federal Election Commission
http://www.fec.gov

League of Women Voters of the United States
http://www.lwv.org

League of Women Voters of Arkansas
http://www.lwv-arkansas.org/

Vote 411
http://www.vote411.org/

Chapter 9

Education

Although the educational process is not usually considered "government" in the ordinary sense of the word, it is one of the major public enterprises of the state with approximately 70% of the state's general revenues (28% of total expenditures) used to support public and higher education.

Except for the section that states that "Congress shall ... provide for the common defense and general welfare of the United States", the United States constitution makes no mention of education. Therefore, since all powers not delegated to the United States are reserved to the states, the establishment and operation of educational facilities is a responsibility of the states. However, over the years, the federal government has provided some funds for education, first in the form of grants of lands that could be used or sold for support of education, and then later (especially in the 1970s and early 1980s), in scholarships and grants for specific purposes such as school lunches, vocational and adult education, special education and rehabilitative services, bilingual education, scientific research, humanities and arts programs, environmental education, etc. In general, however, the operation and financing of the public schools and public higher education is left to the states.

Legislative Milestones

When Arkansas became a territory in 1819, no governmental effort was made to organize an educational system, although Arkansas was the beneficiary of the provisions of a United States ordinance of 1785, which allocated to new territories and future states "lot #16 of every township for the maintenance of public schools within said township." The Constitution framed at the time Arkansas became a state in 1836 professed great admiration for education and the first governor, James Conway, in his inaugural address urged the General Assembly to develop a system of public schools. An act of the U.S. Congress in 1843 gave the Arkansas state government expanded use of the "sixteenth-section lots" by allowing counties to sell them and establish endowments for schools. Unfortunately, very little action was taken to implement this act and few schools were built.

In This Chapter

Legislative Milestones

Constitutional Provisions

General Education

Workforce Education

Higher Education

Comparison to Other States

Terms to Know

desegregation

general education

higher education

"separate but equal"

workforce education

Almost nothing was done about schools during the Civil War or during the reconstruction years following the war. The legislature of 1868 did, however, create the necessary machinery for a public school system, including an office of state superintendent of public instruction, a state board of education, county superintendents, districts, and trustees. Black and white students were to receive education in separate schools. Following the adoption of the Constitution of 1874, a new law was passed encompassing much of the 1868 law and also providing for the levy of taxes to support the public schools.

The history of support for higher education in Arkansas is similar to that of support for the public schools. As with the public schools, the United States Congress passed legislation that provided funding opportunities for higher education, but, like most states, Arkansas failed to take full advantage of these opportunities. The 1785 ordinance which provided that the 16th section of every township be set aside for the public schools was followed in 1787 by an ordinance which set aside two to four townships in the new territories and states of the United States for support of universities. In 1827, Congress passed an act reserving two entire townships of public lands in Arkansas "for the use and support of a university within said territory, and for no other purpose whatsoever." Unfortunately, for a variety of reasons, including difficulty with marketing the lands, Arkansas did not succeed in selling the property in a manner that would have provided an adequate endowment for a university.

The United States Congress gave further support to higher education when it passed the Morrill Act in 1862, which provided for the establishment of one "land-grant" college or university in each state. Land-grant colleges were required to emphasize the "agricultural and mechanical arts" (A&M) in their curricula. To benefit from this act, Arkansas needed to have its land-grant college in operation by February 12, 1872. In 1871, the legislature passed "An Act for the Location, Organization, and Maintenance of the Arkansas Industrial University, with a Normal Department Therein." The Board of Trustees established by this act met in September, 1871, and after much debate about the location of the university, the state succeeded in meeting the February, 1872, deadline with the establishment of the University of Arkansas at Fayetteville (formerly Arkansas Industrial University) and in 1873, the University of Arkansas at Pine Bluff (formerly Branch Normal Arkansas AM&N College).

Constitutional Provisions

The Constitution of 1874 states that "Intelligence and virtue being the safeguards of liberty and the bulwark of a free and good government, the State shall ever maintain a general, suitable and efficient system of free public schools and shall adopt all suitable means to secure for the people the advantages and opportunities of education." Over the years, several amendments to the constitution have dealt with education. Amendment 40 removed the property tax millage limit that local school districts could propose for approval by the voters. The Constitution of 1874 had provided "that all persons in the state between the ages of six and 21 may receive gratuitous instruction," but Amendment 53 allowed public funds to be spent on education for those under six and those over 21, thus permitting public funding of kindergartens and adult education. Amendment 33 gave constitutional independent status to the boards of trustees of institutions of higher education. Amendment 52 provided for establishment of community colleges. Amendment 44, known as the "interposition" amendment, directed the General Assembly "to take appropriate action and pass laws opposing in every Constitutional manner the Unconstitutional desegregation decisions of May 17, 1954, and May 31, 1955, of the United States Supreme Court..." Adoption of this amendment was to haunt Arkansas education for many years since it formed the legal basis for opposition to desegregation efforts and was at least partially responsible for the federal courts holding the state liable for costs of desegregation of local school districts. After federal courts ruled Amendment 44 "null and unenforceable," Arkansas citizens voted in 1990 to repeal it.

General Education

General education in Arkansas underwent historic changes in 2003-2004 as a result of a decade-old class action lawsuit and a subsequent court ruling. The Lake View School District in Phillips County, the lead plaintiff in the suit, challenged the equity of the state's school funding formula. In November of 2002, the Arkansas Supreme Court ruled that the state's system for funding general education was "inequitable" and "inadequate," thus making it unconstitutional. To address the ruling, Governor Mike Huckabee called a special session of the Arkansas General Assembly that began in December of 2003 and lasted 61 days, making it one of the longest extraordinary legislative sessions in modern history. The legislators' efforts resulted in:

- a new funding formula, which sends an extra $439 million a year to school districts, including $132 million for districts that have large numbers of low-income students (Act 59 of 2004)

- an increase in the teacher-salary pay scale and an increase in first-year teacher minimum starting salaries (Act 59 of 2004)

- the consolidation of district administrations with fewer than 350 students (Act 60 of 2004)

- an increase in the state sales tax rate from 5.125% to 6% to generate more funding for education (Act 107 of 2004)

- more standardized testing and tracking individual student progress from grade to grade (Act 35 of 2004)

- a new accounting system that is more standardized and thorough in tracking school district spending (Act 61 of 2004)

- a so-called "doomsday" provision, which gives education spending priority over spending for all other state agencies (Act 108 of 2004)

The Arkansas Supreme Court appointed two masters to review the outcomes of the special session. After the 2007 legislative session, the special masters reported that the legislature had complied with the court rulings, had established a constitutionally acceptable school finance system (including state support for facilities), and had processes in place to continue to provide adequate resources for schools in the future. The Arkansas Supreme Court adopted the report and closed the case.

The State Board of Education has general supervision of the public schools of the state and is responsible for implementing legislation passed by the General Assembly. The board's responsibilities include development of standards for accreditation of schools and of teachers, curriculum development and promotion, selection and distribution of textbooks, development of programs for teacher training, supervision of operation of school budgets, and development of specifications for construction of schools. The board also sets standards for the use of media services, educational television, and volunteers; for involvement of the public; for record keeping and reporting; for equal educational opportunities; for special education and gifted and talented programs, and for cooperation among school districts. In addition, the board must "perform all other functions which may now or hereafter be delegated to the State Board of Education by law." (A.C.A. 6-15-401) The board is further charged with organizing the General Education Division as necessary "to perform all proper functions and render maximum service relating to the operation and improvement of the general education programs of the state." In accordance with Act 855 of 1999, the board must include two members from each of the state's four congressional districts along with one at-large member. The governor appoints members for seven-year terms.

The Department of Education carries out and enforces State Board of Education standards and policies for students in kindergarten through grade 12. Although they do not function as part of the Department of Education, the budgets of the Educational Television Commission (AETN), the State Library, the Arkansas School for the Blind, the Arkansas School for the Deaf, and the Department of Workforce Education are included in the Department of Education's annual budget. Each of these affiliate agencies has its own board or commission responsible for supervising their operations.

School Districts and School Boards. There are nearly 250 school districts and school boards in Arkansas. Arkansas law states that "there shall be only one kind of school district in this state, and each shall have the same prerogatives, powers, duties, and privileges..." (A.C.A. 6-13-101) Each school district has rights and responsibilities as a corporate body, each has the power of eminent domain, and each operates under directives from an elected board of directors. The size of school boards varies from five to nine members. In the 1993 legislative session, the General Assembly enacted Act 786, which generally requires all school districts with a 10% or more minority student population to elect school board members from five or seven single-member districts or five members from single-member districts and two at large positions. The law's objective is to provide more opportunity for minority representation on school boards. Act 786, however, does not apply to districts which are already demonstrating compliance with the Federal Voting Rights Act of 1965, as amended. Boundaries of school district zones are determined by the county election commission. The districts must have "substantially equal population based on the most recent available census information and from which racial minorities may be represented on the board in proportions reflected in the district population as a whole." In most districts, school board members serve three-year terms of office.

The responsibilities of the school boards include providing for care and custody of school buildings and property; providing adequate school facilities; employing teachers and staff; assuring that all subjects prescribed by the state board of education are taught; keeping of accurate records and making appropriate reports; exercising fiscal management and budget responsibilities; and doing "all other things necessary and lawful for the conduct of efficient free public schools in the district." They are also charged with "visiting the schools frequently, seeing to the welfare of the pupils, encouraging them in their studies, and assisting the teacher in the work so far as they can." Each year, at least 25 days before the annual election, the board is required to publish in a county newspaper (at least once a week for three consecutive weeks) an estimate of the amount of money needed by the district for the ensuing year, including the amount needed for general control, instruction, operation and maintenance of the facilities, auxiliary services, fixed charges, capital outlay, and debt service. If the board decides that additional revenues are needed, it is the board's responsibility to estimate the amount of millage required, and to arrange for the millage request to be placed on the ballot. Until 1988, the annual school elections were held in March, but the date was changed to the third week in September.

Educational Standards. In 1983, in order to provide all children in Arkansas with quality education, the General Assembly passed Act 445, "The Quality Education Act of 1983", which provided for a 15 member Education Standards Committee to recommend to the State Board of Education new standards for accreditation of Arkansas public schools. These standards were adopted in 1984 and became officially effective June 1, 1987. After that date, the Department of Education was required to review annually the status of each school district and to notify those districts that were failing to meet the minimum standards. The law states that schools that continue to fail to meet standards must be eliminated. A school district operating one or more schools that fail for two years to meet standards must be dissolved and annexed to another district which operates schools that are all in compliance. If the school board of a school district affected by such action believes the State Department of Education determined improperly that the district had failed to meet standards, that district has the right of appeal to the State Board of Education.

In cases where a district is not meeting standards, the State Board of Education may direct its consolidation with another school district, or, if the school district is too isolated to be combined with or annexed by another district, the board may provide for additional funds to help such a district comply. Act 445 also provided for school districts to annex or combine voluntarily in order to meet standards. The minimum standards adopted by the Board of Education include:
- curriculum standards
- instruction standards regarding class size, teaching load, textbooks and instructional materials, discipline, school calendar, homework and independent study, extracurricular activities, and requirements for participating in extracurricular activities
- attendance and immunization requirements
- requirements for student performance and graduation requirements
- teacher certification and teacher evaluation
- standards for administrators, counselors, and other personnel

In 1991, the educational standards were expanded by Act 236 entitled "Meeting the National Education Goals: Schools for Arkansas' Future." This act was based on

goals set by President George Herbert Walker Bush and the states' governors. It states that, by the year 2000:
- all children in America will start school ready to learn
- high school graduation rate be increased to at least 90%
- students leaving grades four, eight, and twelve demonstrate competency in English, mathematics, science, history, and geography
- U.S. students are to be first in the world in mathematics and science
- every adult is to be literate and possess necessary skills and knowledge to compete in a global economy and exercise rights and responsibilities of citizenship
- every school is to be free of drugs and violence and offer a disciplined learning environment conducive to learning

The act further directed the General Education Division of the Department of Education, with the assistance of the National Alliance for Restructuring Education, to develop a plan for accomplishing these goals.

In 1999, Act 999 established the Arkansas Comprehensive Testing, Assessment and Accountability Program (ACTAAP). It includes the Smart Start Initiative, which focuses on Grades K-4; the state's Smart Step Initiative, which focuses on Grades 5-8; and the state's Smart Future enhanced curriculum program for Grades 9-12. The state is also obligated to uphold standards outlined in the federal No Child Left Behind Act of 2001.

Education Service Cooperatives. In order to promote cooperation among school districts, the General Assembly, in 1985, passed legislation authorizing the State Board of Education to establish a statewide system of multi-county education service cooperatives. The 15 cooperatives now in existence receive some funding from the state, but also receive funds from the schools they serve based on the cost and amount of services provided. The cooperatives give schools the opportunity to share staff and equipment in order to meet the education standards more easily. They may pool funds to provide in-service training for teachers and school personnel that individual schools cannot afford. The Department of Education uses the cooperatives for distribution of materials and information and sends specialists trained in such fields as special education, compensatory education and reading.

Consolidation. In 1912, there were 5,143 school districts in Arkansas. Today there are nearly 250. Over the years, the General Assembly has passed numerous laws regarding consolidation of school districts. Among the most recent laws was Act 811 of 1989 which expanded the reasons for which a school district could be dissolved or merged. Any school district which had less than 85% of its students meeting certain standards on the basic competency test was required to participate in a school improvement program administered by the Department of Education. If the district fails to make "reasonable progress" in improving those test scores within two years of the establishment of the program, that district may be dissolved and merged with another district. In 1991, Act 966 was passed to compile most of the consolidation laws into one subchapter of the Arkansas Code to simplify the consolidation process. It also required county boards of education to seek the attorney general's opinion on the impact of any proposed consolidation or annexation on the effort of the state to assist districts in school desegregation.

As mentioned earlier, consolidation was one of the key issues during the 2003-2004 special legislative session. The General Assembly passed Act 60, which required districts with fewer than 350 students to merge administrations by July 1, 2004.

Minimum Foundation Program Aid. State financial aid to the public schools is distributed according to a complicated formula called the Minimum Foundation Program Aid formula. This formula is based on each school district's "weighted" ADM (average daily membership). The ADM is defined as "the total number of days attended (by students) plus the total number of days absent by students in grades kindergarten through twelve each school day during the first three quarters of each school year, divided by the number of actual days taught during that period." (A.C.A. 6-20-302) The term "weighted" refers to the "add-on" weights given a school district for programs for special education, vocational education, and the gifted and talented. In 1989, the General Assembly passed legislation which gave "add on" weights to those school districts that participated in voluntary consolidation. "Credit allowances" are given school districts for all certified personnel holding a master's or higher degree. Also factored in are a school district's local resources. These resources are based on the assessed value of property available for taxing. A district with low local resources receives more aid than one which has high local resources (primarily based on local property tax assessments). During a special session in early 2004, the General Assembly passed Act 59, which modified the funding formula to achieve more "equity" among the state's school districts.

Educational Excellence Fund. In 1991, the General Assembly established the Educational Excellence Trust Fund into which all funds earmarked for education are deposited. These funds are then distributed to higher education and to the public schools. Although most state aid to the public schools is distributed according to the formula of the Minimum Foundation Program Aid, other funds are set aside by legislative action for new vocational education programs, aid to the handicapped, compensatory education (remedial education), adult education, and apprenticeship programs.

Textbooks. Free textbooks and other instructional materials are provided for all pupils attending the public schools, grades 1-12. The Board of Education is responsible for establishing appropriate guidelines in regard to the adoption, purchase, and distribution of text books. Not later than March 15 of each year, the Director of the Department of Education appoints, with Board of Education approval, "selecting" committees to review textbooks and other materials and to recommend those they believe should be approved for use it Arkansas schools. Each committee has nine members and is composed primarily of classroom teachers but may also include administrators and curriculum directors. There are eight selecting committees, each reviewing a different curriculum area. These areas are: language arts, social studies, science, mathematics, computer science, practical arts, foreign languages, and special education. One or two selecting committees meet each year, but each curriculum area is covered only once every five years. The committees' recommendations are presented to the Board of Education by the director for approval. Each year a list of approved textbooks and instructional materials is sent to the school boards of the local school districts, which then have the responsibility for deciding which of these books will be used in the district. Those decisions are usually reached in consultation with school administrators and teachers.

School Personnel. It is the responsibility of the local school districts to employ superintendents, principals, teachers, department heads, coaches, and other certified personnel, by written contract, for a period of not more than three years. The law states that no classroom teacher may be employed who is not licensed to teach in Arkansas. Teachers are required to take nationally recognized tests in the subject area they teach to become certified.

School Attendance. All children between the ages of five and 17 must be enrolled in a public, private, or parochial school or be provided a home school in accordance with home school laws. There are two exceptions to this requirement. One is for a person who has already received a high school diploma or its equivalent. The second involves kindergarten attendance. Parents and guardians may elect for their child not to attend kindergarten by filing a signed kindergarten waiver form with the local school district superintendent.

Enrollment requirements for parents and guardians who choose to send a child to a public kindergarten changed when Act 462 of 2007 was adopted. For the 2009-2010 school year, students may enter kindergarten in the public schools of Arkansas if the student will attain the age of five (5) years on or before September 1, 2009. For the 2010-2011 school year, students may enter kindergarten in the public schools of Arkansas if the student will attain the age of five (5) years on or before August 15, 2010. For the 2011-2012 school year and afterwards, students may enter kindergarten in the public schools of Arkansas if the student will attain the age of five (5) years on or before August 1 of the year the student is seeking initial enrollment.

Although private schools and parochial schools operate without state funds and are not required to be certified, they may request accreditation by the North Central Association, a long-standing non-governmental organization that lends official approval to academic institutions of various types.

State law requires that all public and private schools display the United States flag. All students attending public or private schools must have proof of required immunizations.

For children to be educated in home schools, parents or guardians must give written notice to the superintendent of the school district in which they reside that they intend to provide a home school for their child. This must be done each year and must be filed by August 15 for the fall semester and December 15 for the spring semester. This notice must include the location of the home school, the basic core curriculum to be offered, the proposed schedule of instruction, and the qualifications of the parent/teachers. Students enrolled in home schools must be tested annually by May 1 using a nationally recognized standardized achievement test. Whenever the test scores of a child eight years of age or older are below the minimum standards established for his or her age, that child must be enrolled in a public, private, or parochial school the following year, unless, prior to the beginning of that year, the student retakes the test and achieves a passing score. In 1999, the Home School Office was added to the Department of Education to promote collaboration between home school parents, public schools, and the department.

Desegregation. Problems connected with the desegregation of Arkansas public schools have frequently dominated the educational scene in Arkansas. Until the *Brown v. Board of Education of Topeka* United States Supreme Court decision of 1954, the public schools of Arkansas operated under the philosophy of "separate but equal." However, following the Supreme Court decision, the National Association for the Advancement of Colored People (NAACP), in February of 1956, filed suit to have 33 black children admitted to previously all-white Little Rock schools. That same year, an initiated petition was circulated to place on the November ballot an amendment to the Arkansas constitution. The amendment would nullify federal actions that were considered encroachments on the sovereignty of Arkansas and would authorize the General Assembly to enact laws to insure enforcement of the amendment. In November, the people of Arkansas approved Amendment 44 by a vote of 185,374 for and 146,064 against. In 1957, when nine black students tried to enter Little Rock Central High School, Governor Orval Faubus called out the Arkansas National Guard to prevent the desegregation efforts, but federal troops were sent in by President Eisenhower to protect the students. Little Rock schools were closed in 1958-59 to avoid desegregation, but opened again in August, 1959, with three black students assigned to Central High and three to Hall High.

Cross-city busing began in 1971. By 1981, black students comprised 64% of the Little Rock School District, because many white students had moved into the Pulaski County or North Little Rock School Districts, or chose to attend to private schools. In November of 1982, the Little Rock School District sued to force consolidation of the three Pulaski County school districts. The federal judge ruled that the three should be consolidated, but his ruling was overturned on appeal. The case continued in the courts until 1989, when the three districts reached a settlement and the General Assembly agreed to pay the financial assessment assigned to the state. In December of 1990, the Eighth Circuit Court of Appeals approved the settlement agreement and dismissed the State of Arkansas from the case.

Workforce Education

Administration. The Department of Workforce Education oversees programs and services in the areas of secondary career and technical education, adult education, and rehabilitative education. The State Board of Workforce Education and Career Opportunities includes seven members appointed by the governor subject to confirmation by the Senate. Act 803 of 1997 requires the appointment of one member from each congressional district and three members from the state at large. The members are to be selected from among parents, business, industry, labor, persons with disabilities, minorities, and other groups representative of the career opportunities available in the state. The directors of the Department of Education and the Department of Higher Education serve as ex-officio members, and the director of the Department of Workforce Education serves as ex-officio secretary.

Secondary Career and Technical Education. The Department of Workforce Education oversees the following career and technical education curricula in secondary education: Agriculture Science and Technology; Business and Marketing Technology; Family and Consumer Sciences Education; Medical Professions Education; Technical and Professional Education; General Cooperative Education; Coordinated Career Education; Principles of Technology; Career Orientation; Workplace Readiness; and Coordinated Compensatory Vocational Education.

The department also administers various programs for special populations and provides access to funding sources for the following secondary career and technical education programs:

Arkansas Construction Industry Craft Training Program – enhanced construction industry craft education at the apprentice and post-secondary levels.

Arkansas Technical Careers Student Loan Forgiveness Program – incentives for Arkansans to enter and complete designated technical programs that meet the demand for employees in various technical occupations.

High Schools That Work – an initiative of the Southern Regional Education Board (SREB) to help raise career and technical students' achievement levels in reading, math, and science.

High-Tech Scholarship Program – $250 per semester for high school graduates who demonstrate exceptional academic and leadership skills and who plan to enroll in a high-tech post-secondary program.

Jobs for Arkansas Graduates – extra help for students enrolled in career and technical education programs to ensure high school graduation and either meaningful employment or post-secondary education thereafter.

Special Needs Programs – special projects and adaptive equipment for secondary and post-secondary career and technical education students with disabilities.

Tech Prep 2+2 Grants – awards for consortia of secondary and post-secondary institutions to articulate two years of secondary education with two years of post-secondary education in a technical program.

Youth Apprenticeships – supplemental work-based learning component to programs of study that involve at least three years of secondary and post-secondary education.

Adult Education. The Department of Workforce Education is also responsible for education programs that provide basic skills classes to adults with less than a high school diploma and who function up to the eighth grade level. Most of these programs are offered free of charge in all 75 counties at local adult education centers.

General Education Development Testing Program – preparation for adults seeking the General Education Development (GED) credential, which is equivalent to a high school diploma.

English as a Second Language Program – English language instruction for adult speakers of other languages.

Workforce Alliance for Growth in the Economy – local alliances of adult educators and employers that identify the competency skills needed in the community's existing and future workforce.

Food Stamp Employment and Training Program – assistance for able-bodied food stamp recipients who have no dependents or who have dependents at least six years of age to find employment and/or enroll in adult education programs.

Governor's Dislocated Worker Task Force – funding for staff to attend community meetings, conduct worker assistance workshops and assessment tests, and provide counseling to dislocated workers.

Rehabilitation Services. A third area the Department of Workforce Education oversees is Rehabilitation Services, which provides vocational training and education and independent living services for people with disabilities.

General Field Program – services designed to assist individuals with disabilities in obtaining and keeping employment.

Hot Springs Rehabilitation Center – a residential facility that provides comprehensive rehabilitation programs, including: live-in accommodations, personal and vocational evaluation, employability services, vocational training, and job placement assistance.

Office for the Deaf and Hearing Impaired – independent living services for persons who are deaf or hard of hearing.

Supported Employment – an integrated work program with ongoing support for individuals with the most severe disabilities.

Services for Persons with End Stage Renal Disease – provided by the Arkansas Kidney Disease Commission to people with end stage renal disease and to people who have received a kidney transplant.

Supported Housing – identifies funding sources for low income, accessible housing.

Technology Access for Persons with Disabilities / Increasing Capacities Network – a federally funded program designed to make technology information available and accessible to Arkansans with disabilities.

Arkansas Consortium for Employment Success – expanded employment opportunities for individuals with physical or mental disabilities, or both, who receive public support.

Creative Alternatives for Delta Area Transportation – employment-related transportation to individuals with disabilities in the Mississippi River Delta region in Arkansas.

Telecommunications Access Program – telephone equipment for eligible individuals.

Arkansas Assistive Technology Alternative Financing Program – gives Arkansans with disabilities access to below-market-rate extended term loans for the purchase of assistive technology.

Higher Education

State supported institutions of higher education in Arkansas include 11 four-year public universities, 22 two-year public colleges, and 12 independent colleges and universities. Each of these universities and colleges has a governing board of trustees responsible for its general supervision and operation. Amendment 33 to the Arkansas Constitution gives these boards a degree of independence by prohibiting their abolition or the transfer of any of their powers. Neither the governor nor the General Assembly may change the composition of a board, and a board member may be removed "for cause only, after notice and hearing."

A law of special interest to citizens of Arkansas is one that waives tuition fees at all public institutions of higher education for individuals 60 years of age or older. (A.C.A. 6-60-204)

The Arkansas Department of Higher Education serves as the administrative staff for the Arkansas Higher Education Coordinating Board. The board consists of nine members who are appointed by the governor and serve staggered seven-year terms. It is responsible for promoting "a coordinated system of higher education in Arkansas" and assuring "an orderly and effective development of each of the publicly supported institutions of higher education." Specifically, it is charged with:
- developing an integrated program of goals
- requesting and receiving information from the higher education institutions
- establishing uniform definitions
- recommending funding levels to the governor and the General Assembly
- reviewing bond issues

The Higher Education Coordinating Board has the power to recommend termination of existing degree programs and approval of new degree programs. In the case of existing programs, the board may recommend a program be eliminated because it overlaps programs taught at other universities or because it fails to meet pre-determined standards. If the board decides a program does not meet the standards, it may place the program on a two-year probation status. If the program cannot meet standards during that time, the board recommends its termination and recommends that no funding be made available for its continuation. In the case of proposed new programs, the board has the responsibility to review new programs to determine whether the units are justified and merit funding. A university is prohibited from spending state revenues on programs not recommended by the board. The board may also give administrative assistance in areas such as federal grants, administration of trusts and endowments, personnel policies and administration, student fees, and transfer of students and of credits. The board is responsible for establishing purchasing criteria and standards for data processing equipment and has authority over higher cost purchases or leases of equipment.

The Higher Education Coordinating Board plays an important role in the budgeting process. Arkansas law gives to the board the power "to review, evaluate, and coordinate budget requests for the state-supported universities and colleges, and to present to the General Assembly and the governor prior to each regular session of the General Assembly a single budget containing the recommendations for separate appropriations to each of the respective institutions." (A.C.A. 6-61-209)

Four-Year Public Universities in Arkansas	
University	Location
Arkansas State University (ASUJ)	Jonesboro
Arkansas Tech University (ATU)	Russellville
Henderson State University (HSU)	Arkadelphia
Southern Arkansas University (SAUM)	Magnolia
University of Arkansas, Fayetteville (UAF)	Fayetteville
University of Arkansas, Fort Smith (UAFS)	Fort Smith
University of Arkansas, Little Rock (UALR)	Little Rock
University of Arkansas for Medical Sciences (UAMS)	Little Rock
University of Arkansas, Monticello (UAM)	Monticello
University of Arkansas, Pine Bluff (UAPB)	Pine Bluff
University of Central Arkansas (UCA)	Conway
Source: Arkansas Department of Higher Education	

Two-Year Public Colleges in Arkansas	
University	Location
Arkansas Northeastern College (ANC)	Blytheville
Arkansas State University, Beebe (ASUB)	Beebe
Arkansas State University, Newport (ASUN)	Newport
Arkansas State University, Mountain Home (ASUMH)	Mountain Home
Black River Technical College (BRTC)	Paragould
Cossatot Community College of the University of Arkansas (CCCUA)	DeQueen
East Arkansas Community College (EACC)	Forrest City
Mid-South Community College (MSCC)	West Memphis
National Park Community College (NPCC)	Hot Springs
North Arkansas College (NAC)	Harrison
Northwest Arkansas Community College (NWACC)	Bentonville/Rogers
Ouachita Technical College (OTC)	Malvern
Ozarka College (OZC)	Melbourne
Phillips Community College of the University of Arkansas (PCCUA)	DeWitt/Helena/Stuttgart
Pulaski Technical College (PTC)	Little Rock
Rich Mountain Community College (RMCC)	Mena
South Arkansas Community College (SACC)	El Dorado
Southeast Arkansas College (SEARK)	Pine Bluff
Southern Arkansas University Tech (SAUT)	Camden
University of Arkansas Community College, Batesville (UACCB)	Batesville
University of Arkansas Community College, Hope (UACCH)	Hope
University of Arkansas Community College, Morrilton (UACCM)	Morrilton
Source: Arkansas Department of Higher Education	

Independent Colleges and Universities in Arkansas	
College or University	Location
Arkansas Baptist College (ABC)	Little Rock
Central Baptist College (CBC)	Conway
Crowley's Ridge College (CRC)	Paragould
Harding University (HU)	Searcy
Hendrix College (HC)	Conway
John Brown University (JBU)	Siloam Springs
Lyon College (LC)	Batesville
Ouachita Baptist University (OBU)	Arkadelphia
Philander Smith College (PSC)	Little Rock
Shorter College (SC)	North Little Rock
University of the Ozarks (UO)	Clarksville
Williams Baptist College (WBC)	Walnut Ridge
Source: Arkansas Department of Higher Education	

Comparison to Other States

Education continues to be one of the most important functions for state governments. In fact, K-12 and higher education spending is the largest item in many state budgets. A key educational dimension is providing enough resources for this enterprise.

Much has been written concerning Arkansas' efforts to deal with school finance issues. As noted earlier, the Arkansas state legislature met in special session to address the ramifications of the Lake View ruling. It is important to note that Arkansas is not the only state that has faced school funding litigation. According to the National Conference of State Legislatures, almost all states have faced legal challenges to the nature and level of funding provided to public schools.

Moreover, the issues raised in these suits are consistent across the states. Initially, the suits focused on the "equity" of state funding. That is, the primary concern was the disparity between rich and poor districts. Wealthy districts spent much more per pupil and provided many more extra-curricular opportunities for their students. Even if poorer districts paid higher property taxes, they did not generate the same level of revenue and therefore did not have the same level of per-pupil expenditures. State court rulings began to address this spending gap in the 1970s. These suits encouraged state legislatures to develop plans that would redistribute state resources to narrow the funding difference among the school districts.

As illustrated in the Lake View case, state courts have presented a new issue for state education funding, and that issue is "adequacy." These cases present a different challenge to the legislative bodies. Rather than focusing on the available funds for education, these cases require state legislatures to provide evidence that the education funding level will provide students with an adequate education.

It is interesting to note that experts disagree about the ramifications of these concepts. Some analysts argue that equity is the more appropriate standard. They contend that fairness dictates that all students receive the same level of per pupil expenditure, regardless of their school district. Moreover, some note that equal per pupil expenditures is a standard that citizens can understand and use to critique the state's funding plan. That is, data can be provided that allow state residents to compare the per pupil expenditures across districts. Citizens can see whether the spending gap is closing between districts, as well as the size of any funding disparity.

Others see great promise in the recent court rulings concerning adequacy. They contend that this idea shifts the focus from distribution of available resources to a more important concern – making sure students receive the training and skills necessary to participate in society. Of course, this raises concerns for some evaluators. Since the primary question is no longer equal distribution of available resources, these rulings may require significant tax increases to achieve an adequate education. In addition, some contend that adequacy can be a moving target that may never be reached. Still others see the adequacy standard as a tool to avoid the demand for equal funding among all pupils.

School expenditures and education quality continue to be important policy questions for all states and governmental officials. As noted earlier, Arkansas is not alone in its efforts to address these issues. Moreover, Arkansas must continue to adjust to new demands and changing legal standards that relate to public education.

Additional Resources

Arkansas Department of Education
http://arkansased.org/

Arkansas Department of Higher Education
http://www.adhe.edu

Arkansas Department of Workforce Education
http://dwe.arkansas.gov

Finance

One of the most important activities of government leaders is setting priorities by the allocation of money. Much of the conflict that occurs between the various governmental branches is based upon disagreements over spending preferences. Whether this clash is between a governor and a state legislature or a mayor and a city council, finances are usually a primary issue in these struggles. This is understandable, because no government has enough resources to provide all of the programs and services requested by the citizenry. Moreover, leaders can disagree about the most pressing financial needs. Tradeoffs and compromise are essential elements in resolving these conflicts.

Under the federal system of government, responsibility for the provision of public services is shared among national, state, and local levels of government. To carry out these functions, each level of government is empowered through a variety of constitutional and legislative mechanisms to collect various types of revenues and to make appropriations for their expenditure.

Constitutional Provisions

The legal foundation of state and local government taxation in Arkansas is the state constitution. Article II (Sec. 23) provides that the "state's ancient right of taxation is herein fully and expressly conceded; and the General Assembly may delegate the taxing power to the extent of providing for their existence, maintenance and well being, but no further." The state uses this taxing authority to raise funds to support its activities, the most significant of which are education, human services, transportation, and the administration of government. There are only two ways in which state tax law can be changed – through actions of the General Assembly or by a statewide referendum. Local tax changes may be made only on authority of the constitution or by delegation of such power by the General Assembly.

Chapter

10

In This Chapter

Constitutional Provisions

State Government Finance

Local Government Finance

Comparison to Other States

Terms to Know

ad valorem tax

Budget Stabilization Trust Fund

consumer sales tax

gas and motor excise tax

intergovernmental sources of revenue

personal and corporate income tax

Revenue Stabilization Law (Act 750 of 1973)

All tax changes and all appropriations must be made within limits set by the Arkansas Constitution. The most relevant sections include:

- "The general appropriation bill shall embrace nothing but appropriations for the ordinary expenses of the executive, legislative, and judicial departments of the State. All other appropriations shall be made by separate bills, each embracing but one subject." (V, 30)

- "No state tax shall be allowed, or appropriation of money made, except to raise means for the payment of the just debts of the State, for defraying the necessary expenses of government, to sustain common schools, to repel invasion and suppress insurrection, except by a majority of two-thirds of both houses of the General Assembly." (V, 31)

- "None of the rates for property, excise, privilege or personal taxes now levied shall be increased by the General Assembly …except by the vote of three-fourths of the members elected to the General Assembly." (Amend. 19, Sec. 38)

Section 38 of Amendment 19 (also called the Futrell amendment) is particularly significant, because it provides that an increase in the rate of any tax in existence in 1934 requires a three-fourths vote to pass. Income, severance, and certain excise and privilege taxes were in existence in 1934, but sales and use taxes were not. As a result, this disparity in voting requirements has served to facilitate the passage of sales and use taxes while hindering the passage of other types of taxes. During legislative sessions, Amendment 19 is the source of a considerable amount of parliamentary and legal arguments about just what is and what is not constitutionally exempt from the three-fourths vote requirement and what is and what is not a rate increase.

Another important constitutional amendment is Amendment 47, adopted in 1958, which states that "no *ad valorem* tax shall be levied upon property by the State of Arkansas." (Sec. 1) This amendment expressly prohibits the state from enacting *ad valorem* taxes on property, thus reserving this mode of taxation exclusively for counties, municipalities, and other sub-state jurisdictions.

State Government Finance

Revenue. State government revenue categories include general, special, intergovernmental, and cash funds. General revenues come primarily from state taxes, including income taxes, sales and use taxes, severance taxes and taxes on alcohol, tobacco, and racing. Special revenues are those collected for specific purposes and may not be transferred to general revenues, such as fees and license money collected by the Highway and Transportation Department and the Game and Fish Commission. Intergovernmental revenues are federal government resources granted to the state. Cash funds come primarily from fees charged by licensing boards and commissions for examinations, permits, and licenses.

Total State Revenues	
Source	% of Total
Personal and Corporate Income Tax	21%
Consumer Sales Tax	20%
Gas and Motor Carrier Tax	3.5%
Other Taxes	6%
Intergovernmental	38%
Other Revenue	11.5%
Source: DFA Office of Accounting, *Comprehensive Annual Financial Report*, 2008	

Personal and Corporate Income Tax - revenues collected from citizens and corporate entities based upon their taxable income as defined by the Internal Revenue Service and Arkansas law. Revenue collected is distributed to state agencies in accordance with the Revenue Stabilization Act and is used primarily for the Departments of Education, Health, Human Services and Correction.

Consumer Sales Tax – revenues collected from consumers on the purchases of goods and services, as proscribed by Arkansas law. This revenue is also distributed to state agencies in accordance with the Revenue Stabilization Act.

Gas and Motor Carrier Excise Tax – special levies on the purchase of motor fuels and certain vehicle related transactions. This revenue is used to fund the Arkansas Highway and Transportation Department.

Other Taxes – special taxes as defined by Arkansas law. These funds are often called special revenue and include such levies as a timber tax in support of the Arkansas

Forestry Commission and are collected for the operations of specific state agencies or programs.

Intergovernmental – predominately federal revenue used to fund federally mandated programs or to support federal grants. Most federal funds utilized in Arkansas are matched by state funds in order to maximize resources.

Other Revenue – sometimes called "cash funds," this revenue is collected through the sale of licenses, tuition, fees, permits, goods, services, investment income, fines and other items. The revenue is collected for the operation of specific state agencies or programs, the most significant of which is the state's institutions of higher education.

The Budget Process. Before any of the general revenues can be expended, the funds must be budgeted. The state budgeting process is shared by agency representatives, the governor, the Offices of Budget and Personnel Management in the Department of Finance and Administration (DFA), the Legislative Council, the Joint Budget Committee of the General Assembly, and the General Assembly.

The governor and the Office of the Budget begin the process by preparing an executive budget. This is sent to the Legislative Council and the Joint Budget Committee, which conduct hearings to review the agencies' proposals and to concur with the executive recommendations or make their own recommendations to the General Assembly. When the General Assembly meets in regular session, the Joint Budget committee assumes responsibility for introducing appropriation bills, reviewing legislative amendments, and making the final "do pass" recommendations. Following passage of an appropriation bill by both houses of the legislature, the appropriation is subject to the governor's approval or veto, including the authority for line-item vetoes.

Revenue Stabilization Law (Act 750 of 1973). The actual distribution of general revenues in Arkansas is governed by the Revenue Stabilization Law, first enacted in 1973 and reenacted each legislative session. This law serves three important purposes: first, it ensures the prohibition of deficit spending; second, it allows the governor and the General Assembly flexibility in setting priorities given the financial resources predicted for the state; and third, it allows the state to move quickly to cut expenditures in the event of a revenue shortfall.

Before the Revenue Stabilization Law, taxes were earmarked for various programs regardless of their needs or the need for new programs. Under this law, state general revenues are pooled and distributed among state agencies according to a rigorous formula. And in contrast to most other states, the governor does not need to call special sessions of the General Assembly for purposes of passing new appropriation bills to adjust to the changes in revenue receipts. Each agency can make budgetary decisions consistent with revenue collections by referring to the revenue stabilization law allocations.

State and Federal Budget Concepts Contrasted. In Arkansas, "appropriations" made to the various departments by the General Assembly are maximum authorizations to spend. The federal counterpart of the state's "appropriation" is "authorization." A state appropriation is not the same as a federal authorization. The latter concept commits or obligates the federal government to certain expenditures. The state concept does not. Like the federal "authorization," the state's "appropriation" approves the programs to be funded.

The Revenue Stabilization Law establishes the maximum that can be spent, but the portion of the state's "appropriation" that is actually available for spending is dependent upon the structure of the Revenue Stabilization Law and the general revenue collections. The Revenue Stabilization Law is the equivalent of the federal concept, except for one crucial difference: the state can spend only available revenues. It must maintain a balanced budget and thereby must set priorities in its spending. The federal government is under no such constraint.

Revenue Stabilization Process. Under the Revenue Stabilization Law, state appropriations are placed in at least three levels of priority spending: "A," "B," and "C" categories. Sometimes "A1" and "B1" categories are also used. In general, "A" priority appropriations are funded, "B" categories are funded when revenues exceed anticipated revenues, and "C" category items are seldom funded.

The Office of Economic Analysis and Tax Research in the Department of Finance and Administration prepares the official revenue forecast for the annual legislative/budgeting cycle. This forecast attempts to predict the total size of the general revenue resources. Under the Revenue Stabilization Law, the governor and the legislature attempt to divide up that total fairly.

Before distribution of revenues under the Revenue Stabilization Law, some revenues are deposited in the Constitutional and Fiscal Agencies Fund, which finances the offices of the state's elected officials (executive, legislative, and judicial), their staffs, and the Department of Finance and Administration. By law, all general and special revenues are deposited with the state treasurer and placed in the General Revenue Allotment Account or the Special Revenue Allotment Account according to the type of revenue being deposited. From the General Revenue Fund, 3% of all general revenues are first deposited in the Constitutional and Fiscal Agencies Fund, and the balance is used to pay the state's obligatory debts (tax refunds, general obligation bonds, mandated or court-ordered expenses) and distributed to the departments, agencies, boards, and commissions as established by the Revenue Stabilization Law. From the Special Revenue Fund, 3% of all special revenues collected by DFA and 1.5% of all special revenues collected by other agencies are deposited in the Constitutional and Fiscal Agencies Fund. The balance is distributed to the agencies for which the special funds were collected.

Budget Stabilization Trust Fund. Another fund in the state's financing process is the Budget Stabilization Trust Fund. Since state revenues are not collected through the year in a pattern consistent with program and agency expenditures, a stabilization fund was established. This fund receives one half of the interest earnings from state funds invested by the state treasurer. (The other half of the interest earnings goes to the state's capital improvement fund.) The Budget Stabilization Trust Fund is then used to manage the cash flow to the various agencies and departments.

Expenditures. Once an appropriation has been passed and revenues have been placed in the appropriate fund, agencies may begin the process of spending. When an office, department, agency, board, or commission incurs an expense, it sends a voucher to the Office of Accounting at the Department of Finance and Administration. That office's pre-audit section checks to be sure there are adequate funds in the budget for such expenditures. If so, it stamps approval on the voucher and sends it to the state auditor who writes a warrant (payment by check). That warrant is returned to the agency which had the expense. That agency sends the warrant to the creditor, and the warrant is redeemed by the state treasurer.

In the case of an agency that receives cash funds, the disbursing officer of the agency (not the auditor) writes the warrant and a bank (not the treasurer) redeems the warrant. A potential exception to this process during budgetary shortfalls is that K-12 education must be funded before all other state services. (Act 108 of 2004)

Audit of Expenditures. At the end of every fiscal year, the Division of Legislative Audits reviews the expenditures of state agencies and prepares audit reports. These reports are submitted to the Joint Auditing Committee of the General Assembly. That committee reviews the reports and makes appropriate recommendations.

Total State Expenditures	
Function	% of Total
General Government	10%
Education	28%
Health and Human Services	44%
Transportation	3%
Law, Justice, and Public Safety	5%
Recreation and Resources Development	2%
Regulation of Business and Professionals	1%
Debt Service	1.5%
Capital Outlay	5.5%

Source: DFA Office of Accounting, *Comprehensive Annual Financial Report*, 2008

General Government – the state's constitutional offices, the General Assembly, the Department of Finance and Administration, various state employee retirement systems, and aid to municipal and county governments.

Education – primary, secondary, and post-secondary public schools.

Health and Human Services – services provided by the Department of Health and the Department of Human Services.

Transportation – projects and services provided by the Arkansas Highway and Transportation Department.

Law, Justice, and Public Safety – services provided by the Arkansas State Police, Arkansas Department of Correction, and various judicial functions.

Recreation and Resource Development – programs and services provided by the Game and Fish Commission, Arkansas Industrial Development Commission, Arkansas Department of Parks and Tourism, and Arkansas Department of Heritage.

Regulation of Businesses and Professionals – programs and services provided by the Arkansas Department of Workforce Services and a multiplicity of licensing and regulatory agencies, boards, and commissions.

Debt Service – repayment of bonds and other state debts.

Capital Outlay – infrastructure and other capital improvements.

Local Government Finance

Local governmental entities in Arkansas – counties, municipalities, school districts, and special improvement districts – primarily get revenue from property taxes and sales taxes.

State and Local Relations. Legally, local governments are creatures of state government. Therefore, the state greatly influences local government tax rates, bonded indebtedness, and balanced budgets. Moreover, one of the largest sources of local revenue is state turnback monies. For all these reasons, local governments are inherently influenced by state policies and financial decisions.

For example, counties are required to provide for the administration of justice through the courts and for law enforcement protection. Although the state pays the salaries of general jurisdiction judges, court reporters, and prosecuting attorneys, salaries of other court employees and other expenses must be paid by the counties. Counties must provide for jail facilities, but such facilities must meet state and federal standards that include restrictions on the number of persons per cell, separation of the sexes and of juveniles, separation of those accused of violent sex crimes, exercise space, outside lighting, access to medical and legal assistance, and visitation rights.

Counties and municipalities also face increased costs to ensure the public health of their citizens due to adoption of environmental standards regulating landfills, sewage treatment and water purification facilities, incinerators, and power generating plants.

School districts must provide for adequate school facilities and safe school buses. They must ensure that the schools in the district meet accreditation standards such as limitations on class size, certification of teachers, offering of specified curricula, and provisions for handicapped and talented students. School districts must also comply with federal laws requiring integrated schools. Failure of a county, city, or school district to comply with federal and state mandates and standards may invite lawsuits that result in court-ordered expenditures.

Bonds. Although the state may, with the approval of the voters, issue certain types of bonds, most bonds are issued by counties, school districts, and especially by municipalities. Bonds are issued for capital improvement projects and may be general obligation or revenue bonds. General obligation bonds must be approved by the electors and may be repaid by property taxes, but those property taxes may not exceed limits established by the constitution and its amendments. Most revenue bonds require approval by the electors, but Amendment 65 authorized "any governmental unit to issue revenue bonds for the purpose of financing all or a portion of the costs of capital improvements of a public nature, facilities for the securing and developing of industry or agriculture, and for such other public purposes as may be authorized by the General Assembly." Furthermore, the General Assembly "may, but shall not be required to, condition the issuance of such bonds upon an election." (Sec. I)

Ad Valorem Taxes. Since passage of Amendment 47 in 1957, local governmental entities have had exclusive right to use the ad valorem property tax. In Arkansas, this tax is levied on both real and personal property, although passage of Amendment 71 in 1992 removed household property from taxation. The Constitution of 1874 states that "all property subject to taxation shall be taxed according to its value, that value to be ascertained in such manner as the General Assembly shall direct, making the same equal and uniform throughout the State. No one species of property from which a tax may be collected shall be taxed higher than another species of property of equal value." (XVI, 5) However, Amendment 57 allowed the General Assembly to classify intangible personal property for assessment at a lower percentage of value than other property and to exempt certain classes of intangible property. Amendment 59 allowed further variations to the requirement that all property be taxed "equally and uniformly." It stated that "residential property shall be assessed in accordance with its value as a residence, so long as said property is used as the principal place of residence of the owner" (Sec. 15a) and that "agricultural land, pasture land, timber land, residential and commercial land, excluding structures thereon, used primarily as such, shall be valued for taxation purposes upon the basis of productivity or use." (Sec. 15b)

Arkansas law states that the assessed property value "shall not exceed 20% of the true and full market or actual value" nor shall it be less than 18%. If it falls below 18% in a certain locality, it is required that the amount of state turnback to that county or city be reduced. The constitution limits the amounts of millage counties and municipalities may levy, but does not limit the amount school districts may levy, though such levies must be approved by the voters.

The *ad valorem* tax is levied at a fixed rate in terms of mills per thousand dollars of the assessed value of property. For example, if the actual value of a piece of property is $100,000, then its assessed value would be $20,000 ($100,000 x 20%). If the *ad valorem* millage rate is $.070 (70 mills x $.001), then the *ad valorem* tax on this property would be $1,400.

Because millage rates are based on the value of property, the process of assessment is critical to proper evaluation of property and to the amount of tax revenue a given amount of millage will produce. Although the Assessment Coordination Department of the state sets guidelines for assessing property, the actual assessing is done by the 75 county assessors. This decentralized structure allows for significant inequities across the state, and these inter-county disparities have not gone unnoticed.

In 1978, the Alma School District and others filed a suit charging that property taxes were not being assessed equally and uniformly across the state as provided for by the Arkansas constitution. The Pulaski County Circuit Court decided in favor of the school district, and the Arkansas Supreme Court upheld their decision. The Arkansas Supreme Court ordered the Assessment Coordination Division to devise an orderly procedure whereby, beginning in 1980, 15 counties per year should be reassessed using court-approved manuals that based appraisals on full market values to assure equitable assessments throughout the state. It was immediately apparent that, in most counties, the new assessments would be so much higher than the old ones that taxes would rise to an unacceptable rate. Therefore, in 1980, the voters approved Amendment 59 which rolled back the amount of increase in tax revenue to 10% above the revenues received during the previous year. There were numerous special provisions in Amendment 59 that have caused implementation to be complicated and interpretations of the amendment to be challenged in the courts. Redress of assessed property values continues to raise questions and controversy.

County Revenues and Expenditures. The constitution and its amendments limit the ad valorem tax counties may levy. The millage rates of these taxes are subject to the limitations discussed earlier for all ad valorem taxes. All millages must be approved by a vote of the people except the millage for general operations and roads, which can be levied by vote of the county quorum court. A county must apportion at least one-half of the revenue it receives from the road tax collected from within municipalities back to the municipalities of the county for use in building and repairing the streets and bridges in their respective cities and towns.

County Ad Valorem Millage Allowable Under Arkansas Constitution			
Amount	Use	Implementation	Authority
5 mills	General Operations	Vote of Quorum Court	XVI, 9
3 mills	Roads	Vote of Quorum Court	Amendment 61
**	Local Capital Improvement Bonds	Vote of the people	Amendments 62, 65
1 mill	Hospital Maintenance	Vote of the people	Amendment 32
5 mills	Library	Vote of the people	Amendments 38, 72
5 mills	Industrial Development	Vote of the people	Amendments 49, 62
**The limit of bonded indebtedness secured by property taxes may not exceed 10% of the total assessed value of real and personal property in a county. Amount of millage is not limited, but must be approved by vote of the people.			

Before passage of Amendment 59, most counties had levied the full five mills for general operations and full three mills for roads, but since reassessment, most counties levy less than the maximum allowed.

Other major sources of revenue for counties are the sales tax and fees, fines, licenses, and charges for services rendered. In 1981, the General Assembly passed legislation allowing counties, with approval of a vote of the people, to levy up to a two per cent sales tax or use tax on sales made within the county. This sales/use tax applies to all products and services that are taxed by the state sales tax. However, for any single transaction, $25 is the maximum tax that may be collected. The revenue collected from this tax is divided between the county and the incorporated cities of the county on a per capita basis.

In the past, fees had been used as a basis of compensation for county officials. However, in 1975, the General Assembly declared that all fees, fines, penalties, and other monies collected by any county officer, deputy, or county employee must be deposited with the county treasurer for credit to the county general fund. Today, the counties collect considerable revenue from fees for marriage licenses, for recording deeds and mortgages and for serving summons, as well as from court costs, fines, and penalties. These fees are set by law and cannot be increased without action by the General Assembly. Fees may also be charged for services provided by the county, such as solid waste collection and disposal, fire protection, and emergency medical services. The amount of these fees is set by the county quorum court.

County operations also depend on general turnback from the state and turnback for roads. Seventy-five percent of the turnback is divided equally among the 75 counties, with the remaining 25% divided on the basis of population. State aid for roads comes primarily from motor fuel taxes, motor vehicle registration and license fees, and title transfer fees. The state returns 15% of these revenues to the counties. This 15% is distributed as follows (Act 371 of 1989):

- 31% is divided according to area, with each county receiving the proportion that its area bears to the area of the state;
- 17.5 % is divided according to the amount of state motor vehicle license fees collected the previous year, with each county receiving a proportion of the total that it bears to the total collected;
- 17.5 % according to population with each county receiving the proportion that its population bears to the state's population;
- 13.5 % according to a county's rural population, and its proportion to the total population of the state; and
- 20.5 % divided equally among all 75 counties.

Although counties may spend state aid on public transportation, the amount spent may not be more than 20% of state aid received.

Quorum courts are required to adopt budgets before the end of each year for the next year. No expenditure may be made without an appropriation. Counties are audited each year by the Division of Legislative Audit.

Municipal Revenues and Expenditures. The procedures and limitations for levying the ad valorem tax by municipalities are similar to those for counties. Except for the five mills for general operations, which may be levied by ordinance of a city or town's governing board, all *ad valorem* tax levies require approval by a vote of the electors of the city or town.

In general, analysts do not encourage municipalities to use property taxes. One reason is that a sales tax can generate greater revenue for the city. Also, if a city raises its property millage, this might encourage people to move out of the city and into outlying areas to avoid higher property taxes.

A major source of revenue for municipalities is the sales tax. Cities and towns have several options in levying a sales tax. The first option is participation in the county sales tax, in which case a city or town receives its per capita share of the revenue received. Use of revenue from the county sales tax is unrestricted. A second option is that any city or town may levy a municipal sales tax on retail sales within the municipality for general purposes or for the purpose of "acquiring, constructing, and equipping of capital improvements of a public nature" or of issuance of bonds for the financing of such capital improvements.

Municipal Ad Valorem Millage Allowed Under Arkansas Constitution			
Amount	Use	Implementation	Authority
5 mills	General Operations	Vote of governing body	XII, 4
**	Local Capital Improvement Bonds	Vote of the people	Amendments 62, 65
5 mills	Industrial Development Bonds	Vote of the people	Amendment 62, 65
1 mill	Firemen's Pension/Relief Fund	Vote of the people	Amendment 31
1 mill	Policemen's Pension/Relief Fund	Vote of the people	Amendment 31
5 mills	Library	Vote of the people	Amendments 30, 72
** The limit of bonded indebtedness secured by property taxes may not exceed 20% of the total assessed value of real and personal property in municipality. Millage not limited, but must be approved by vote of the people.			

In addition, first class cities may levy up to three per cent sales tax upon the gross receipts of hotels and restaurants (the so-called "hamburger" tax). Use of revenue from this tax must be used for recreation, the advertising and promoting of the city, or for construction, repair, or operation of a convention center. The levy of any sales tax must be approved by a vote of the people, and if financing of bonds is involved, the voters must approve their issuance. Any city levying a hotel and restaurant sales tax must create a city Advertising and Promotion Commission to oversee the expenditure of the revenue received.

Other taxes that municipalities may levy include privilege, franchise, and occupation taxes, alcoholic beverage licenses and taxes, and taxes on motor vehicles, amusement devices, and aviation fuel.

With approval of the voters, municipalities may also levy a tax on the income of the residents who work in a city but live outside its taxing area. Some large municipalities who have a significant number of employees living outside its boundaries have presented this tax as a revenue option.

Fees for services and other charges also comprise a significant source of income for municipalities. Sanitation, utility, water, and sewer fees, emergency service charges, inspection fees, dog licenses, and parking meter charges are used to provide the services for which the charges are made.

Revenue also comes from the fines and court costs charged by city courts. The fines are used to pay for operation of the courts and other city operations, but most court costs are mandated by state law for special purposes, such as education of judges and clerks, University of Arkansas law schools, law libraries, judges and state police retirement funds, alcoholic rehabilitation programs, public defenders, and others. Increasingly, court costs amount to such large sums that fines are not imposed or are very small.

General turnback is allocated among the cities on a strictly per capita basis. Municipalities also receive 15% of the state's highway revenues in the form of street turnback. Street turnback, like general turnback, is allocated on a per capita basis. Cities of over 50,000 may use up to 10% of such turnback for public transportation, and up to 20% if under 50,000.

Cities must adopt annual budgets and are required to have their financial affairs audited annually either by an independent certified public accountant or by the Division of Legislative Audit of the state.

School District Revenues and Expenditures. As with the counties and municipalities, school districts receive revenue from the federal government, from state government, and from local taxes. In recent years, the federal portion has declined, and the local portion which is mostly ad valorem taxes has increased only slightly. Consequently, school districts have been forced to depend more and more on the state portion.

Federal revenues are generally limited to support for the school lunch program, some entitlement funds for compensatory education services (remedial education programs), supplementary materials, and education of handicapped children. Local tax revenues are limited by the amount of school millage voters are willing to approve. Although there is no constitutional limit on the amount of millage that may be levied for schools, the property tax is an especially unpopular tax and millage proposals are often rejected.

Improvement Districts and Authorities. Other entities with taxing powers include improvement districts and authorities created under state law for special purposes. Improvement districts have been formed for the building of levees and drainage control, dam and lake districts, and water districts. Improvement districts are frequently formed in cities or towns for purposes such as housing projects, parks, museums, and arts centers.

Governmental units may act independently or may combine to establish public facilities boards or authorities for such purposes as managing facilities for health care, waterworks, sewers, solid waste disposal, incinerators, recycling facilities, public housing, recreation and park facilities, public transportation, etc. These "authorities" are usually incorporated and have powers that include the right to sue and be sued; to fix, charge and collect rents, fees, and charges; to lend money for the financing of projects; to invest money; and to have general control of the facilities for which they were established. State law provides for appropriate boards to oversee operation of the different projects.

Comparison to Other States

Arkansas' finances share many common traits with those of other states. The typical taxes collected by the U.S. states and local governments are: income, sales, property, gasoline, tobacco, alcohol, severance (natural resources), gambling, and various user fees. Arkansas governmental entities utilize all of these revenue sources.

A distinctive characteristic of Arkansas' tax structure is that it relies more heavily on sales and use tax revenue than other states. As noted earlier, this can be explained by the constitutional limits associated with raising any tax in existence before 1934 (Amendment 19). For example, income tax increases require a three-fourths vote in the state legislature, while additional sales taxes can be adopted by a simple majority vote. There was an attempt to place the same voting requirements for all tax changes made by the General Assembly. However, the Arkansas electorate rejected this proposal.

Another way to compare Arkansas' finances with other states is to look at some common criteria used to evaluate taxes. These criteria are: equity; yield; elasticity; ease of administration; effects on economic behavior; and political acceptability.

Equity focuses on the fairness of a tax. This usually means some kind of assessment concerning the citizen's "ability to pay." Usually equity will contrast progressive taxes (e.g., income tax), where the tax increases as the individual earns more money, with regressive taxes (e.g., sales tax), where lower income residents pay proportionally more of their income in taxes.

Yield is concerned with how much total revenue can be generated by a tax. That is, once the tax is collected and government subtracts the administrative costs, how much money is available to pay for public services. A tax that provides a great deal of revenue with little administrative expense is preferable to a tax that provides moderate revenues with significant managerial expenditures.

Elasticity addresses the adaptability of a tax. This feature examines whether a tax is able to adjust to changing economic conditions. Therefore, taxes that automatically adjust for improving or declining economic circumstances are considered elastic. Moreover, those that do not respond or respond slowly to a different economic climate are considered inelastic.

Ease of administration means that taxes are easy for citizens to understand and can be obtained with minimal effort by the government. Simply put, it should be clear to citizens how much taxes they are required to pay. In addition, government officials should acquire tax revenue in a manner that allows efficient collection without citizens evading their tax assessments.

Effects on economic behavior contends that as a general rule, taxes should not change a citizen's purchasing patterns. For example, if property taxes become so high they prevent an individual from purchasing a new home, these taxes are having an undue impact on economic behavior. It should be noted there are situations where government officials utilize taxes to discourage certain types of activity. That is, the state may raise the sales tax on cigarettes in an effort to discourage smoking.

Political acceptability argues that the various states and local taxes should be in agreement with citizen preferences. Officials know that residents do not want to pay taxes. However, the taxes that are levied by the government should be those that are most acceptable to the populace.

When Arkansas' finances are evaluated using these dimensions, it reveals both strengths and weaknesses in the state taxation system. Since Arkansas relies more heavily on sales taxes, this means the state fares well compared to other states on the criteria of yield, elasticity, ease of administration, and political acceptability. In addition, the availability of personal and corporate income taxes also assists the state concerning three of these elements (equity, yield, and elasticity).

When one examines the state's efforts to generate monies, the use of income and sales tax are key components in this endeavor. That is, income and sales taxes produce a great deal of revenue without large administrative costs, therefore they provide significant tax yields.

Relative to other taxes, income and sales tend to adjust to changing economic conditions. If personal income is increasing, then income tax revenues tend to increase. However, if income is declining then individuals move to lower tax brackets and pay less tax. Sales taxes are not as elastic as income taxes. But relative to property taxes and most other fees, they can more easily reflect changes in the state's economy.

Sales taxes are also relatively easy to administer. The tax is collected when items are sold, and most citizens have a general understanding of their tax burden. Moreover, some aspects of income taxes are easy to administer. Employers withhold the tax from their employees' salaries and the employer sends the money to the state. However, a weakness of income tax assessments is complexity. Many citizens do not know their level of income taxes and would find it difficult to calculate their tax obligation.

Political acceptability is another strength of Arkansas' reliance on sales taxes. In general, the public seems to prefer sales taxes and other user fees to income and property taxes. As noted earlier, sales taxes are clear and the average citizen understands the workings of this tax. For example, people trying to buy a soft drink priced at $.89 know the cost of the drink will be more than this amount. They realize a sales tax is applied to the advertised price of this product, but they would recognize the clerk is overcharging them if told the cost is $1.25.

The greatest weakness of Arkansas' overall tax system, compared to other states, concerns the issue of equity. A sales tax is a regressive tax because it is not based upon the ability to pay. For example, when the wealthy purchase a soft drink for $.89, they pay less of their income in sales tax than a factory worker who makes $20,000 a year. Since equity focuses on the issue of fairness, this shortcoming continues to be an important area of concern for policy makers. However, under current constitutional constraints, state lawmakers may find it difficult to move away from a reliance on sales and use taxes.

Compared to other states, Arkansas is consistently ranked near the bottom on per capita spending. On the other hand, when the U.S. Census Bureau analyzes state and local tax collection as a percent of personal income, Arkansans' tax efforts seem to be proportionally higher than expected.

Overall, financial matters will continue to be a key area of conflict in Arkansas state government. Reasonable citizens can disagree about the relative priority of different initiatives. Moreover, efforts to determine the best way to achieve diverse political goals inevitably lead to clashes among various interests. Finally, state and local governments must estimate their expected revenues and expenditures. When economic circumstances change and there are revenue shortfalls, difficult decisions must be made concerning future budgetary expenditures.

Additional Resources

Arkansas Municipal League
http://www.arml.org

Association of Arkansas Counties
http://www.arcounties.org

Department of Finance and Administration
http://www.arkansas.gov/dfa/

Nelson A. Rockefeller Institute of Government
http://rockinst.org/

Tax Foundation
http://www.taxfoundation.org/

U.S. Census Bureau
http://www.census.gov

APPENDIX A

Amendments to the Arkansas Constitution of 1874

"Amended" refers to laws that have been changed.
"Superseded" means that the existing amendment has been replaced by another.
"Repealed" means that the law is no longer in effect.

Number	Year Adopted	Method Proposed	Subject Matter
1	1880	Legislative	Holford Bonds
2	1898	Legislative	Regulation of transportation
3	1898	Legislative	3-mill county road tax (superseded)
4	1900	Legislative	Sureties on official bonds
5	1912	Initiative	Compensation of legislators (amended)
6	1914	Legislative	Executive Department; lieutenant governor
7	1920	Legislative	Initiative and referendum
8	1920	Legislative	Equal suffrage (superseded)
9	1924	Legislative	Supreme Court (superseded)
10	1924	Legislative	City and county debt limitation (amended)
11	1926	Legislative	18-mill school district tax (superseded)
12	1926	Legislative	Textile mills tax exemption
13	1926	Initiative	Bond issue in cities (superseded)
14	1926	Initiative	Local acts prohibited
15	1928	Legislative	Salaries of state officers (superseded)
16	1928	Legislative	Jury trial
17	1928	Legislative	County construction tax (superseded)
18	1928	Initiative	Tax to aid industries
19	1934	Legislative	Tax increase restrictions
20	1934	Legislative	State bonds (superseded)

21	1936	Legislative	Criminal prosecutions, prosecutor's salaries
22	1936	Initiative	Homestead exemptions
23	1936	Initiative	Board of Apportionment (superseded)
24	1938	Legislative	Chancery and probate matters (amended)
25	1938	Legislative	County building construction (superseded)
26	1938	Legislative	Workers' compensation
27	1938	Initiative	Tax exemption for new industries
28	1938	Initiative	Regulating practice of law
29	1938	Initiative	Filling vacancies in office
30	1940	Initiative	City libraries (superseded)
31	1940	Initiative	Police and firefighters' pensions
32	1942	Legislative	County or city hospitals
33	1942	Initiative	Boards and commissions
34	1944	Initiative	Rights of labor
35	1944	Initiative	Game and Fish Commission
36	1944	Initiative	Poll tax exemption for military (superseded)
37	1946	Legislative	State officers' salaries (superseded)
38	1946	Initiative	County libraries (superseded)
39	1948	Legislative	Voter registration laws (superseded)
40	1948	Legislative	Unlimited school district taxes (superseded)
41	1952	Legislative	Election of county clerks
42	1952	Legislative	State Highway Commission
43	1956	Initiative	Salaries and expenses of judicial officers
44	1956	Initiative	Interposition (repealed)
45	1956	Initiative	Apportionment
46	1956	Initiative	Horse racing and pari-mutuel wagering
47	1958	Legislative	State ad valorem tax prohibition
48	1958	Legislative	Legislative salaries (superseded)
49	1958	Legislative	Industrial development bonds (superseded)

50	1962	Initiative	Voting machines (superseded)
51	1964	Initiative	Voter registration; elimination of poll tax
52	1964	Initiative	Community colleges
53	1968	Legislative	Kindergarten; adult education
54	1974	Legislative	State printing contracts
55	1974	Legislative	Revision of county government
56	1976	Legislative	Salaries for state officers (superseded)
57	1976	Legislative	Intangible personal property
58	1978	Legislative	Court of appeals
59	1980	Legislative	Property reappraisal and millage rollback
60	1982	Legislative	Interest rate control
61	1982	Legislative	County road tax
62	1984	Legislative	Local capital improvement bonds (superseded)
63	1984	Initiative	Four-year terms for constitutional officers
64	1986	Legislative	Municipal courts jurisdiction
65	1986	Initiative	Revenue bonds
66	1988	Legislative	Judicial ethics commission
67	1988	Legislative	Juvenile court jurisdiction
68	1988	Initiative	Abortion funding
69	1990	Legislative	Repeal of Amendment 44
70	1992	Legislative	Salaries for state officers
71	1992	Legislative	Exemption from taxation of household property
72	1992	Legislative	Allowable library millage raised
73	1992	Initiative	Term limits
74	1996	Legislative	Uniform minimum property tax for schools
75	1996	Legislative	Sales tax to support Game and Fish Commission
76	1996	Initiative	Congressional term limits (struck by supreme court)
77	1998	Legislative	Assignment of special and retired judges (superseded)

78	2000	Legislative	City and county government bonds
79	2000	Legislative	Property tax relief
80	2000	Legislative	Revision of judicial article
81	2002	Legislative	Secret ballots
82	2004	Legislative	Obligation bonds for economic development
83	2004	Initiative	Marriage
84	2008	Legislative	Voting, Qualifications of Voters and Electors, and Time of Holding General Elections
85	2008	Legislative	Annual Legislative Sessions and Fiscal Budgeting
86	2008	Initiative	State Lottery

APPENDIX B

Governors of Arkansas

Name	Dates of Service
James S. Conway (D)	1836-1840
Archibald Yell (D)	1840-1844
Thomas S. Drew (D)	1844-1849
John S. Roane (D)	1849-1852
Elias N. Conway (D)	1852-1860
Henry M. Rector (Independent Democrat)	1860-1862
Harris Flanagin (D)	1862-1864
Isaac Murphy (Unionist Democrat)	1864-1868
Powell Clayton (R)	1868-1871
Elisha Baxter (R)	1871-1874
Augustus H. Garland (D)	1874-1877
William R. Miller (D)	1877-1881
Thomas J. Churchill (D)	1881-1883
James H. Berry (D)	1883-1885
Simon P. Hughes (D)	1885-1889
James P. Eagle (D)	1889-1893
William M. Fishback (D)	1893-1895
James P. Clarke (D)	1895-1897
Dan W. Jones (D)	1897-1901
Jeff Davis (D)	1901-1907
John S. Little (D)	1907-1909
George W. Donaghey (D)	1909-1913
Joseph T. Robinson (D)	1913

George W. Hayes (D)	1913-1917
Charles H. Brough (D)	1917-1921
Thomas C. McRae (D)	1921-1925
Tom J. Terral (D)	1925-1927
John E. Martineu (D)	1927-1928
Hanley Parnell (D)	1928-1933
J.M. Futrell (D)	1933-1937
Carl E. Bailey (D)	1937-1941
Homer M. Adkins (D)	1941-1945
Ben T. Laney (D)	1945-1949
Sidney McMath (D)	1949-1953
Francis Cherry (D)	1953-1955
Orval E. Faubus (D)	1955-1967
Winthrop Rockefeller (R)	1967-1971
Dale Leon Bumpers (D)	1971-1975
David Pryor (D)	1975-1979
Bill Clinton (D)	1979-1981
Frank White (R)	1981-1983
Bill Clinton (D)	1983-1992
Jim Guy Tucker (D)	1992-1996
Mike Huckabee (R)	1996-2007
Mike Beebe (D)	2007-present

APPENDIX C

Important Dates in Arkansas Political History

Year	Event
1541	DeSoto and his men cross the Mississippi River into Arkansas (June 18)
1686	Founding of Arkansas Post
1762	France cedes Louisiana (including Arkansas) to Spain
1800	Spain returns Louisiana to France
1803	United States purchase Louisiana from France (April 30)
1819	Territory of Arkansas created (March 2)
1819	Territorial government organized (July 28)
1820	First school established at Dwight Mission, near Russellville
1821	Territorial capital moved from Arkansas Post to Little Rock
1836	Arkansas admitted to the Union as the 25th state (June 15)
1836	State government organized; first Arkansas Constitution (September 12)
1861	Arkansas secedes from the Union; second Arkansas Constitution (May 6)
1864	Third Arkansas Constitution
1868	Arkansas readmitted to the Union; fourth Arkansas Constitution (June 22)
1872	Arkansas Industrial University opens in Fayetteville with eight students (January 22)
1873	Branch Normal College opens in Pine Bluff with seven students (September)

1874	Ratification of the Arkansas Constitution of 1874 (October 13)
1908	First free public library established in Fort Smith
1911	General Assembly meets in new state capitol (January 9); building began in 1900 and was completed in 1914
1918	Defeat of the proposed constitution drafted by a convention in 1917-1918
1932	Arkansas elects first woman to U.S. Senate – Hattie W. Caraway
1935	Arkansas sales tax first enacted into law
1955	League of Women Voters Arkansas established
1955	Arkansas Industrial Development Commission established
1957	Desegregation of Little Rock Central High School (September)
1966	Winthrop Rockefeller elected Arkansas' first Republican governor in 92 years
1970	Defeat of the proposed constitution drafted by a convention in 1970
1980	Defeat of the proposed constitution drafted by a convention in 1980
1984	Voters approve four-year terms of office for Arkansas constitutional officers
1992	Voters approve term limits for state officials
1992	Bill Clinton elected President of the United States
1993	Dr. Joycelyn Elders confirmed as U.S. Surgeon General (September 8)
1996	Governor Jim Guy Tucker resigns
2002	Arkansas Supreme Court rules state public education funding formula unconstitutional
2004	General Assembly mandates consolidation of school districts with less than 350 students
2008	Voters approve change from biennial to annual legislative sessions
2008	Voters approve a state lottery for higher education scholarships
2009	Hillary Clinton confirmed as U.S. Secretary of State

APPENDIX D

Arkansas Congressional Districts

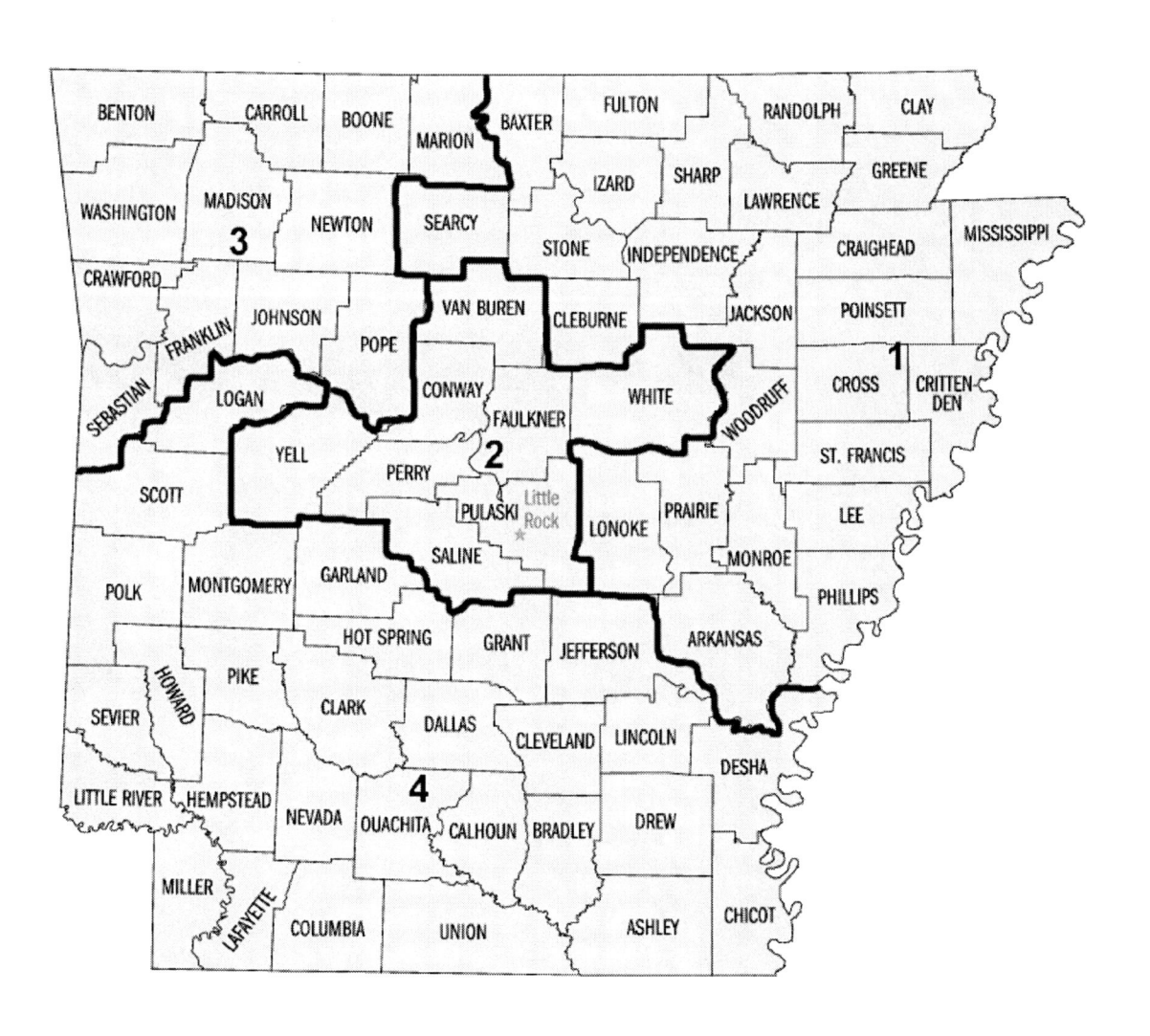

Bibliographic References

Arnold, Morris S. *Colonial Arkansas, 1686-1804: A Social and Cultural History.* Fayetteville, AR: University of Arkansas Press, 1991.

Barnhart, Ralph C. "A New Constitution for Arkansas?" *Readings in Arkansas Government.* Ed. Walter Nunn. Little Rock, AR.: Rose Publishing, 1973. 1-19.

Beyle, Thad L. and Lynn R. Muchmore, eds. *Being Governor: The View from the Office.* Durham, N.C.: Duke University Press, 1983.

Blair, Diane D. *Arkansas Politics and Government: Do the People Rule?* Lincoln, NE.: University of Nebraska Press, 1988.

Bolton, S. Charles. *Arkansas, 1800-1860: Remote and Restless.* Fayetteville, AR: University of Arkansas Press, 1998.

Book of the States 2008. Lexington, KY: Council of State Governments, 2008.

Bowman, Ann M. and Richard C. Kearney. *State and Local Government*, 5th ed. Boston: Houghton-Mifflin, 2002.

Bromeley, Seth. "Masters say school fix needs push." *Arkansas-Democrat Gazette*, 3 April 2004: A1+.

Dougan, Michael B. *Arkansas Odyssey: The Saga of Arkansas from Prehistoric Times to Present.* Little Rock, AR: Rose Publishing, 1994.

Dresang, Dennis L. and James J. Gosling. *Politics and Policy in American States and Communities.* 3rd ed. New York: Longman, 2002.

Dye, Thomas S. Politics in States and Communities. 9th ed. Saddle River, NJ: Prentice-Hall, 1997.

Elections Division, Office of the Arkansas Secretary of State, ed. *Election Laws of Arkansas and Constitution of the State of Arkansas of 1874.* Charlottesville, VA: Matthew Bender & Co., 2001.

Gibson, James L. et al. "Whither the Local Politics?: A Cross-Sectional and Longitudinal Analysis of the Strength of Party Organizations." *American Journal of Political Science* 29 (1985): 139-160.

Greer, Tom and Lavell Cole. *Arkansas: The World Around Us.* New York: MacMillan/McGraw-Hill School Publishing Company, 1991.

Hershey, Marjorie Randon. *Party Politics in America*. 13th ed. Pearson Education, Inc., 2009.

Jewell, Malcolm E. and Sarah M. Morehouse. *Political Parties and Elections in American States*. 4th Edition. Washington, DC: Congressional Quarterly Press, 2001.

Johnson, Ben F. *Arkansas in Modern America, 1930-1999*. Fayetteville, AR: University of Arkansas Press, 2000.

Kellams, Laura. "Legislators get some A's for efforts on schools." *Arkansas-Democrat Gazette*, 8 February 2004: A1+.

Key, V.O., Jr. *Southern Politics in State and Nation*. New York: Random House, 1949.

Nunn, Walter. "The Negativism of the 1874 Constitution" *Readings in Arkansas Government*. Ed. Walter Nunn. Little Rock, AR.: Rose Publishing, 1973. 20-25.

Nunn, Walter, ed. *Readings in Arkansas Government*. Little Rock, AR.: Rose Publishing Company, 1973.

Olson, Mancur Jr. *The Logic of Collective Action: Public Goods and the Theory of Groups*. Cambridge, MA: Harvard University Press, 1965.

Running for Public Office: A "Plain English" Handbook for Candidates. Little Rock, AR: State Board of Election Commissioners, December 1997.

Sabato, Larry. *Goodbye to Good-time Charlie: The American Governorship Transformed*. Washington, DC: Congressional Quarterly Press, 1983.

Schreckhise, William D. and Janine Alisa Parry. "Arkansas." *Legal Systems of the World: A Political, Social, and Cultural Encyclopedia*. Ed. Herbert M. Kritzer. Santa Barbara, CA: ABC-CLIO, 2002. 73-77.

Thomas, Clive S. and Ronald J. Hrebenar. "Interest Groups in the Fifty States." *Comparative State Politics* 20 (1999): 7-13.

Wang, Richard and Michael B. Dougan, eds. *Arkansas Politics: A Reader*. Fayetteville, AR: M & M Press, 1997.

Whayne, Jeannie M., et al. *Arkansas: A Narrative History*. Fayetteville, AR: University of Arkansas Press, 2002.

Whistler, Donald E. and Charles Dewitt Dunn. "Professional and Amateur Lobbyists in the Arkansas Legislature." *Arkansas Political Science Journal* 8 (1987): 27-40.

Index

A

Absentee Voting, 99
Ad Valorem Tax, viii, 71, 79, 130, 137, 138, 140, 141, 148
Administrative Procedure Act, 48
Agriculture Department, 40
Amendment 80, 51, 52, 55, 62, 65, 66, 70
Annexation, 74, 82
Appellate Jurisdiction, 51, 57
Apportionment, 3, 7, 9, 98, 148
Appropriation, 3, 9, 16, 18, 22, 23, 46, 72, 130, 132, 133, 139
Arkansas Building Authority, 40
Arkansas Bureau of Legislative Research, 12, 28
Arkansas Circuit Court Districts list, 61
Arkansas Constitution
   amendment process, 4
   centralization of power and representation, 2
   comparison to other states, 4
   comparison to U.S. Constitution, 4
   Constitution of 1836, 1
   Constitution of 1861, 1
   Constitution of 1868, 1
   Constitution of 1874, x, 2, 3, 5, 69, 70, 112, 113, 137, 147, 154
   constitutional history, 1
   political corruption control, 2
Arkansas Court of Appeals, 56
Arkansas Court Structure (diagram), 59
Arkansas Court System, 55
   Administrative Office of the Courts, 63
   Arkansas Court of Appeals, 56
   Arkansas Supreme Court, 57
   Circuit Courts, 56
   City Courts, 55
   comparison to other states, 65
   District Courts, 55
Arkansas Political History, ix
Arkansas Political History Milestones (list), 153
Arkansas Supreme Court, 23, 26, 34, 47, 52, 56, 57, 63, 64, 69, 113, 114, 138, 154
Attorney General, 9, 23, 24, 30, 35, 48, 65, 118
Auditor, 36, 37, 97, 134

B

Bills, 14
Bills Filed and Laws Enacted in Regular Sessions Since 1961, 12
Boards and Commissions, 45
Bonds, 3, 136, 138, 140, 147
Budget Stabilization Trust Fund, 134
Bureau of Legislative Research, 21

C

Campaign Financing, 106
Circuit Clerk, 70
Circuit Courts, 56
City Administrator Form of City Government, 78
City Courts, 55
City Manager Form of City Government, 76
Civil Cases, 52, 54, 55
Classification, 75
Clemency, 31
Clincher Motion, 17
Committee Organization, 17
Committees

interim, 20
joint, 18
select, 18
standing, 18
Commutation of Sentences, 31
Congressional Districts, 155
Constable, 71
Constitutional Officers, 29
Coroner, 71
Correction Department, 41
County Assessor, 71
County Boards, 72, 97, 98, 100
County Clerk, 70
County Collector, 70
County Equalization Board, 72
County Expenditures, 72
County Government, 67
County Judge, 70
County Officers, 69
   circuit clerk, 70
   coroner, 71
   county assessor, 71
   county clerk, 70
   county collector, 70
   county judge, 70
   county surveyor, 71
   county treasurer, 70
   sheriff, 70
County Revenues, 71, 138
County Surveyor, 71
County Treasurer, 70
Court Appointed Special Advocates, 64
Court Case Coordinators, 63
Court Personnel, 62
   case coordinators, 63
   court reporters, 63
   court secretaries, 63
   prosecuting attorneys, 62
   public defenders, 62
Court Reporters, 63
Court Secretaries, 63
Criminal Cases, 52, 54, 63

D

Department of Workforce Education, 121
Desegregation of Arkansas Public Schools, 120
District Courts, 55

E

Early Voting, 101
Economic Development Commission, 41
Economic Development Districts, 80
Economic Interest Group, 88
Education, 111
   adult education, 45, 122
   comparison to other states, 127
   consolidation, 117
   constitutional provisions, 112
   Department of Education, 115
   desegregation, 120, 154
   education service cooperatives, 117
   Educational Excellence Fund, 118
   four-year public universities (list), 125
   general education, 113
   higher education, 43, 121, 124, 125, 126, 127, 128
   independent colleges and universities, 127
   legislative milestones, 111
   Minimum Foundation Program Aid, 118
   rehabilitation services, 45, 123
   school attendance, 119
   school districts and school boards, 115
   school personnel, 119
   secondary career and technical education, 121
   standards, 116
   State Board of Education, 114
   textbooks, 119
   two-year public colleges (list), 126

workforce education, 121
Education, Department of, 42
Elections, 95
  absentee voting, 99
  comparison to other states, 107
  cost, 101
  County Boards of Election Commissioners, 98
  early voting, 101
  in Arkansas, 104
  independent candidates, 105
  nominees, 105
  political practices pledge, 106
  presidential preferential primaries, 103
  primaries, 102
  State Board of Election Commissioners, 97
  violation of election laws, 101
  write-in candidates, 106
Environmental Quality Department, 42
Equal Opportunity Interest Group, 89
Executive Branch, 29
Expenditures, State of Arkansas, 134

F

Families in Need of Services, 56
Finance, 129
  ad valorem taxes, 137
  bonds, 136
  budget process, 132
  Budget Stabilization Trust Fund, 134
  constitutional provisions, 129
  county *ad valorem* millage rates, 138
  expenditures, 134
  improvement districts and authorities, 142
  local governments, 136
  municipal ad valorem millage rates, 140
  revenue, 131
  Revenue Stabilization Law, 132
  revenue stabilization process, 133
  school district revenues and expenditures, 141
  total state expenditures (list), 135
  total state revenues (list), 131
Finance and Administration, Department of, 42
Freedom of Information Act, 48

G

Game and Fish Commission, 43
General Assembly
  apportionment, 9
  bills, 14
  committee organization, 17
  committees, 19
  comparison to other states, 27
  compensation of members, 13
  congressional districts (map), 155
  House of Representatives, 7
  interim organization, 20
  joint resolutions, 14
  occupations of members, 13
  president *pro tempore* of the Senate, 7
  qualifications of senators and representatives, 8
  resolutions, 14
  secretary of the Senate, 7
  Senate, 7
  sessions, 9
  speaker of the House, 7
  term limits, 13
  vacancies, 13
Governor
  budget preparation, 31
  judicial power, 31
  political resources, 30
  preparation, 30
  qualifications, 29
  roles, 31
  special sessions, 31
  term limits, 30
  veto power, 31
Governors of Arkansas (list), 151
Grand Juries, 53

H

Health Department, 43
Heritage Department, 41
Higher Education, 124
Higher Education, Department of, 43, 124
Highway and Transportation, Department of, 44
Home Rule, 67, 69
House Committees (list), 18, 19
How a Bill Becomes a Law in Arkansas, 15

I

Incorporation, 74
Independent Candidates, 14, 105
Information Systems, Department of, 44
Interest Group Resources, 89
Interest Groups, 88
   economic interest group, 88
   equal opportunity interest group, 89
   lobbying, 17, 90, 91, 93
   public interest group, 89
   resources, 89
   strategies and tactics, 90
Intergovernmental Cooperation Councils, 73
Interim Committees, 20
Intermediate Appellate Courts, 52
Interstate Compacts, 81
Intitiative, 22, 26, 69, 79, 117, 147, 148, 149, 150

J

Joint Committees, 18
Joint Committees (list), 19
Judicial Branch, 51
Judicial Selection, 52
Judiciary Concepts, 51
  appellate jurisdiction, 51
  civil cases, 52
  criminal cases, 52
  grand juries, 53
  intermediate appellate courts, 52
  judicial selection, 52
  original jurisdiction, 51
  petit juries, 53
  supreme courts, 52
  trial courts of general jurisdiction, 51
  trial courts of limited jurisdiction, 51
Justice of the Peace, 8, 69, 71

L

Labor Department, 44
Lake View School District Case, 113
Land Commissioner, 37
Legislative Council, 20
Legislative Joint Auditing Committee, 21
Legislative Procedures and Rules, 14
Legislative Sessions, 9
Lieutenant Governor, 7, 30, 33, 34, 104, 147
Local Government, 67
  comparison to other states, 82
  county government, 67
  municipal government, 73

M

Mayor-Council Form of City Government, 75
Merit System, 39
Municipal Boards and Commissions, 79
Municipal Expenditures, 79
Municipal Government, 73
Municipal Government Forms, 75
Municipal Revenues, 79, 140

N

National Conference of State Legislatures, 28, 127

O

Organization of State Government, 40
Original Jurisdiction, 51, 52, 56, 57, 70

P

Pardons, 31, 81
Parks and Tourism, Department of, 44
Party Nominees, 105
Petit Juries, 53
Petitions, 5, 14, 22, 23, 24, 25, 26, 35, 57, 74, 75, 77, 78, 79, 82, 85, 105, 120
Planning and Development Districts, 80
Political Parties, 85
   comparison to other states, 92
   county committees and county conventions, 87
   functions, 85
   party organization, 86, 157
   selection of members, 88
   state committees and state conventions, 87
Political Practices Pledge, 106
Presidential Preferential Primaries, 103
Primaries, 102
Prosecuting Attorneys, 62
Public Defenders, 62
Public Interest Group, 89

Q

Quorum Court, 26, 68, 138

R

Recall, 26
Referendum, 22, 24, 26, 69, 79
Referral, 26
Resolutions, 14
Resource Conservation and Development Councils, 81
Revenue Stabilization Law, 132
Revenue, State of Arkansas, 131
Right-to-Work Employment Laws, 39

S

Secretary of State, 9, 23, 24, 31, 34, 35, 48, 74, 85, 97, 105, 106, 107
Select Committees, 18
Senate Committees (list), 19
Sheriff, 70
Solid Waste Management Districts, 81
Special Sessions, 9
Standing Committees, 18
State Agencies, 39
   Agriculture, 40
   Arkansas Building Authority, 40
   Arkansas Heritage, 41
   Arkansas State Police, 41
   comparison to other states, 48
   Correction, 41
   Economic Development Commission, 41
   Education, 42
   Environmental Quality, 42
   Finance and Administration, 42
   Game and Fish Commission, 43
   Health, 43
   Higher Education, 43
   Highway and Transportation, 43
   Human Services, 44
   Information Systems, 44
   Labor, 44
   Office of Personnel Management, 39
   Parks and Tourism, 44
   Workforce Education, 45

Workforce Services, 45
State Board of Apportionment, 9, 35
State Board of Education, 114
State Police, 41
Supreme Appellate Courts, 52

T

Term Limits
   executive branch, 30
   legislative branch, 13
The Arkansas Register, 48
Township Officers, 71
Treasurer, 36, 63, 70, 78, 133, 134, 139
Trial Courts of General Jurisdiction, 51, 55
Trial Courts of Limited Jurisdiction, 51, 55

V

Veto, 24, 31, 70, 73, 76, 77, 78, 132
Voter Registration, 96
Voting Rights in Arkansas Constitution, 96
Voting Rights in U.S. Constitution, 95
Voting Rules, 95

W

Workforce Education, 45, 115, 121, 122, 123, 128
Workforce Education, Department of, 45
Workforce Services, Department of, 45
Write-In Candidates, 106